The Psychoanalysis of Everyday Life

sometimes I pee when I laugh

D1111687

A Collection of Humorous Observations

by

Sheli Ellsworth

BeachHouse Books

Chesterfield Missouri USA

The Psychoanalysis of Everyday Life: sometimes I pee when I laugh Copyright © 2012 by Sheli Ellsworth.

BeachHouse Books

for Jeff...

       the funniest straight

       man I ever loved.

Prologue

I hope you enjoy the stories. At some point in life, I decided to give up my quest for perfection and enjoy the process of living. For me it meant seeing the humor in everyday situations. It took a while for the idea to take hold, but once it did, I think I became a better person.

I also hope you can identify with some of the absurdity we call life. And I hope that someday if you are bitten by a squirrel, overrun by rabbits or trapped on the toilet that you too will see the humor in it.

Feel free to contact me at

justsheli@yahoo.com.

Stories

Plump shiny lips anyone?

Cursed with a tendency to have chapped lips, I've embarked on a lifelong journey to cure this medical mystery. In an effort to buy down my karmic debt and better my fellow man, I'm sharing my success and failures.

I became aware that my lips were different from others when I was sixteen and working in a department store. It was winter, and the warm forced-air heating had dried my lips into two piecrust-like slices. Desperate for relief, and unable to leave my workstation, I searched under the checkout counter until I found an almost-new jar of Vaseline. I carefully applied a small amount of the jelly. Within minutes the pain had subsided. Proud of my brilliant ingenuity, I mentioned the Vaseline cure to my middle-aged co-worker, Joanna. She looked somewhat surprised, and readily informed me that Sylvia, another hormonally challenged co-worker, used that jar of Vaseline for her hemorrhoids.

Yuuuk! I immediately considered a lipectomy to excise the contamination from my skin or shock therapy to erase it from my brain? During my break, I raced to a drug store, like the mother of twins down to the last diaper, to buy Listerine, Lysol, flea shampoo, and anything that might wash the image of the large woman's sphincter from my brain.

If *post-traumatic-petroleum-syndrome* wasn't bad enough, I still had dry lips. Eventually, I made a bold decision to go across the department store to the cosmetic counter, where I had found a longwearing, plumping vitamin E lipstick. It was like finding out that ice-cream is healthier than broccoli. The shiny display cases flaunted several glamorous shades and seduced me into buying what appeared to be the perfect solution to my dry-cracked dilemma. I selected a subtle coppery color that complimented my pale complexion. The next morning it went on smoothly; the color looked perfect in my bathroom mirror. Then I caught a glimpse in the dressing room mirror at work. It appeared that the soft copper gloss had turned a deep pinkish purple with the dubious side effect of giving my lips the crusty finish once again.

Entering a neurotic stage of denial, I convinced myself that poor lighting was the cause of the apparent color transformation. I'd used the poor lighting excuse before—it was the only way I could shop for bathing suits. This fantasy lasted until lunch, when I discovered that not only were my lips rather dry and purple, but they were also absurdly swollen. I appeared to be the victim of a rare allergy called *necrostupidosis*. I went into the ladies room and using hand soap, attempted to scrub the dye from my swollen lips. When this did not work, I tried hand sanitizer, only to find that this actually contributed to the plumping, drying process.

I spent the next two days averting my gaze from all forms of reflection, and fearing I would be mistaken as the first place winner of a pie-eating contest at a country fair somewhere in Iowa, married to a guy named Bubba.

Continuing to seek out lip concoctions for the next few years, I discovered that sunscreen, tequila, kissing, and a few things I won't go into only aggravated the problem. Timing was also important. Applying a lip balm right before I went to sleep made a big difference in overall kissability and cosmetic appearance, although anything that promised to "soothe" or had a tiger on the label turned out to be a huge mistake. But moving the lip treatment du jour to my nightstand was genius.

One morning, my sleepy eyes caught sight of a pair of blue lips staring back at me from the medicine cabinet mirror. I was sure I'd developed a rare form of cyanosis. The thought of seeking medical help frightened me. Was I dying? I looked closely, wondering if my doctor could treat this, or would I need an internist, allergist, or even an OBGYN! Should I rush to the emergency room while I was still conscious? I finally came out of my stupor long enough to run my finger across the blue surface. It was sticky. I grabbed a tissue. Some of the blue gummy stuff came off. I charged into the bedroom opening the small drawer. There, to my relief, I found several sticks of zinc oxide sunscreen in neon colors that I'd purchased on a recent trip to Australia.

After considering the ridiculousness of my prior panic, I broke into clown-like grin—cracking my lips once again.

One-ply low flow way-to-go

Until lately, I thought the only people who dwelt on toilet paper issues were companies like Procter and Gamble, Mr. Whipple, and those crazies who write to Dear Abby about proper dispensing. However, recent events have led me to change my opinion of the one-ply versus two-ply debate.

I should've known that toilet paper wasn't to be taken lightly after visiting relatives brought in their own ultra plush, ultra soft version of the same brand I already had. And, like religion and politics, it wasn't discussed in polite company. However, when our toilets started to plug up regularly, we could no longer ignore the obvious.

Hardly a day went by when our plunger didn't have to be used. We trained our children in the use, cleaning, and storage of the tool of shame. However, there were certain refinements of its utility they failed to master. Don't leave it on the counter next to the toothbrushes, don't hand it to visiting guests, and don't use it to play tug-of-war with the dog.

Finally, our plumber diagnosed the problem. Low flow, environmentally friendly toilets combined with high-end two-ply was terminal. We had no choice. Cheaper paper was the only answer.

I was one of the many who'd bought into the whole *soft* propaganda campaign, knowing full well people once used catalog pages for the same purpose. But, we're a sophisticated society, as evidenced by soft cuddly cartoon grizzlies that sell us the overpriced necessity in 30-second increments on television. Now I'd have to wander into the seedy underworld of low-end tissue.

Once in the warehouse supply store, I was relieved not to see anyone I knew. I kept my sunglasses on—just in case. I headed down aisles like I owned a cheap motel next to an All-You-Can-Eat Hot Wings Buffet. No one would know I'd stooped so low. Once there, I was shocked to find so many brands of low-rent pulp.

I selected one based on weight. I'd heard that trick from an old TP expert. It was 100% organic, evidence by the gray color. I purchased a 48-roll package, not the equivalent of 48 rolls, but 48 actual rolls. It was heavy. I felt like I was getting my $11.69 worth and then some. I rolled it out to the parking lot on a handcart with my jacket collar pulled high around my face.

At home, I was amazed how quickly I filled the bathroom cabinets. I began to stuff rolls in every nook and cranny. I was surprised how much wasted space was in the kitchen and office cabinets. Now, if I could just remember where it was when I needed it.

I didn't have to wait long to find out how my experiment was working. Two days go by—no clogs. On day three, I optimistically sanitized and stowed the plunger.

Day four. My teenage daughter came down stairs and asked me why we had truck stop toilet paper. I explained that many truckers suffer from hemorrhoids and truck stop paper is generally much nicer than ours is. She left the room with an indignant air.

Day seven. My teenage son asked me what

happened to our TP (he is a little slow sometimes). "We've switched to a more environmentally friendly product," I told him.

"Mom, that's no answer. That stuff is awful!"

"Once you get used to it, you won't even notice," I said defensively. "People once used corncobs. This is much better than corncobs. Some societies still use leaves. You should feel lucky."

"What kind of leaves? I'm sure they're softer."

"You'll toughen up and before you know it that stuff at school will feel spa soft."

"Mom, I don't use the school's TP."

"What do you mean you don't use the school's toilet paper?"

"Mom, Can we just drop it?"

Anyway, they can complain all they want; I've chosen my side of the issue, or should I say tissue?

Sixty-seven days and counting.

The pumpkin master

My husband is not an artistic man. So, when he and our seven-year-old daughter were invited to enter a father-daughter pumpkin carving contest, I was a little skeptical. This was the man who wanted to frame his high school jockstrap and hang it on the wall. His idea of a color pallet was using those red disclosing tablets from the dentist.

However, he and our daughter would spend a Saturday morning at the mall with other father-daughter teams, scooping pumpkin seeds and whittling designs for the final judging at noon. I figured that at least this way, I wouldn't be finding wayward pumpkin seeds all over the house until Christmas.

It sounded like fun . . . but I recalled the year prior, when our pumpkin had no teeth and my husband told our children that pumpkins don't get teeth until puberty. However, they were both excited and I wished them luck.

They returned hours later with no pumpkin. When I inquired, I found out that the pumpkins would be on display for the rest of the day.

"Cool," I said, "a showing!"

"Oh yeah," my husband replied. "You'll have to go see them. Our daughter picked a unicorn design." He rolled his eyes.

"A unicorn," I said in disbelief, recalling the mangled mouth of last Halloween. "Did you win?"

"Oh no, Marilyn Monroe won."

"Isn't she dead?"

"The design was Marilyn—the one with her dress up."

"How did a bunch of dads carve Marilyn Monroe in a pumpkin?" I asked, incredulously.

"The Pumpkin Master helped us."

"The Pumpkin Master?"

"Yeah, the guy had all the designs and just walked us through the whole thing."

"Was there a second place?" I had to know.

"The guy who carved out a headless horseman in 3-D"

"How did he carve out a headless horseman in 3-D?" I said in disbelief.

"With an electric Dremmel tool."

"Is that fair?"

"If you bring your own Dremmel, it is."

"I didn't think it would be so competitive."

"Oh yeah, one guy brought seven small pumpkins and carved out dwarfs."

"Did he win anything?"

"No, it was against the rules. He was really upset. You could only enter one pumpkin."

"Did he leave all seven of the dwarfs for display?"

"Nah—he just left grumpy."

Ladybug lesson

Winter had beckoned lazy aphids into the windowsill planters over my sink. They had flourished, plumping on the kalanchoes who waited patiently for the resuscitation of summer light, which would make their leaves glossy and their flowers bloom. The aphids had never been welcome guests, despite their quiet demeanor and ability to stay confined to the pot. The plants were beginning to show signs of annoyance at the presence of their visitors; several potions, poisons and relocation programs had been unsuccessful.

One source recommended I procure more aggressive aphids that were sensitive to poisons, to eat the current ones, which were not. Fearing a Frankenstein effect, where gargantuan aphids surviving on leftovers would eventually need vaccinations and paper training, I decided

against it.

I recalled that ladybugs have been known to dine on aphids; surely, those friendly creatures would not frighten children or company if they happen to land on a plate of potato salad. I set off to find a few wild ladybugs willing to vacation at my sink-side resort with the free buffet. This turned out to be more difficult than I had expected.

The little dears were nowhere to be found during afternoons, and morning ladybugs proved as elusive as coeds sneaking into dorm rooms. Yes, the proper ladybug was more active in the evening; but flashlights, night vision goggles, and a butterfly net didn't make them easier to catch. These genteel beetles were faster than hookers on payday. By the end of the week, I had two ticks and an earwig. It was time for a more assertive approach.

I began phoning local garden centers and discovered that ladybugs can be purchased just like manure or fungicide. So, I set out to buy the elusive arthropods. The nursery's salesman said they were $7.99 per container. Pretending to be a savvy shopper, I inquired about the number of ladybugs for that price, as if they were t-bones or push-up bras. I was told there were about 1,500 in the pint size container, which looked more like a Ben and Jerry carton than a carnivorous mass of insect superheroes.

"Fine," I replied, while paying the young man and figuring the cost per bug. How did he know how many were in there? And who counted them in the first place?

"Water your yard first and then sprinkle them around in the evening," the salesman directed.

"Thank you," I said, contemplating the small number actually needed to discourage my unwelcome visitors.

Once home, like any consumer, I ignored the salesman's advice and decided to remove a few of the polka dot mercenaries to start on my aphid cafeteria. I walked near the window planter and ever so gently pried up the lid. Immediately, I knew, I was in trouble. Even before the lid was actually removed, a ladybug riot had begun. At least a brigade escaped within a nanosecond. I quickly pushed the lid back down to the sound of crunching, aware that I'd crushed some of the very guests I'd invited.

My heart felt heavy, but only until the little aliens made their way up my arm and onto my clothes. I tried grabbing a few for the

14

short trip to the planter. Unfortunately, the sleek ovoid design of their armor prevented them from capture. In fact, their glossy surface and six-legged death grip made them immune to traditional means of transport. Within minutes, several were flying around the kitchen, landing on every available surface (except the aphid-infested planters). About a dozen found their way into my hair and one was determined to make the sprint between my lips and nose.

The throng crawling on the floor made it difficult to move around the kitchen at all. I grabbed a glossy piece of mail attempting to slip it under the little invaders. But once the Botox ad came near them, they changed direction and crawled up my hand, once again racing up to the protection of my clothes and nose. By this time they were everywhere. I decided that perhaps the technology of the hand vacuum could help, and the survivors could be retrieved from the dirt cup. The only problem was getting from the kitchen to the pantry for the device.

Trying not to step on any of the little creatures, I picked my way across the floor — but several of them scurried under foot, resulting in the same crunch I heard earlier. Some fled the confines of my pant legs with each step, resulting in even more smashed bugs.

Once the squishing began, the floor became slippery which made it even more difficult to avoid the wanderers. By the time I returned from the pantry, the kitchen resembled a sort of indoor slip-n-slide. I began to speculate about what kind of mass murderer this made me — a psychopath or a sociopath. Jeffery Dahmer also invited guests into his home and then snuffed them out. I finally retrieved the small appliance and began to chase them with the noisy transporter device. Many were sucked into the reservoir; however, several were too fat for the ride. Some were clever and clung to rough surfaces. Those who survived my relocation program enjoyed our First Annual Aphidfest. However, a few were still crawling on the ceiling toward the curtains, others were visiting fruits, vegetables, and the even the cookie jar.

I decided to arm myself with a bigger weapon and went to get the big vacuum. I emptied the messy filter from the vacuum labeled "no messy filter" and tried to locate the correct accessory. None of the "on board tool assortment" was labeled "for bugs," so I grabbed one that said "crevices" and went to work.

I began to suck the little *Coleopterans* off the ceiling, the curtains and out of my bra; then I targeted the marauders who had made it onto the fresh tomatoes. I vacuumed the aggressive interlopers from inside the spice cabinet, the top of the trash can, and the bottom of the cat. I finished and removed the dust cup. A few were in the catch-22 of the HEPA filter. Some made the trip alive, some did not. A few expired in the house, but the remaining cohorts in the Ben and Jerry container did make the evening show and were released into the backyard at sunset on cool watered grass.

The ladybugs were now children of summer. I was no longer responsible for the care and feeding of an entire civilization. I had done all I could. It was up to them. I had to trust that their wings and their wisdom would be enough. I said good-bye. I was left with an only child in the kalanchoes over the sink.

Days later, my young son found a dead ladybug on the floor. Devastated by the discovery he asked me if we could bury it and say a few kind words. "A funeral," I replied, "it's the least I can do."

Closet of guilt

I recently attempted to clean out my closet— throw things away, donate to charity, and find a skirt that had been missing since '96. It took months for me to work up the courage. Did I really want to know what was lurking behind the rabbit coat I bought in high school? I'd heard fashion expert Stacy London say that if you haven't worn something in the last year it should be discarded. I had a hard time with the one-year time frame.

What if I just got rid of things I hadn't worn in the last decade? Would anyone really know how long I kept my Girl Scout uniform? What if almost everything I owned needed to go?

It had been a while since I'd actually entered my closet. I was pretty happy with my dry-n-fly system where I just stepped into my clothes straight from the dryer as I was ready to go out the door. Granted, my wardrobe had become limited to a couple of pairs of khaki capris and t-shirt that said, "I'm with Stupid," but if I needed to switch it up I could always grab someone else's t-shirt from the dryer and pretend it was an honest mistake. I bet even Stacy London wore tees? And a hoodie could pull any outfit together.

I started by having a few cups of very strong coffee. If anything went terribly wrong, I could blame it on the caffeine.

The first scary things were the cobwebs. When I noticed all the shoulder pads, I couldn't figure out why the spiders weren't as frightened as I was. Shoulder pads were empowering. Elaine on Seinfeld wore the ubiquitous padded shoulder jackets. Elaine was assertive and she had really bad luck with men. Maybe if you have a loud mouth you shouldn't wear padded shoulders. I think Elaine ruined it for all of us. The first order of business was to remove anything that looked like it might have an ex-boyfriend wearing it.

Once I'd removed the tailored, button down masculine crowd, I headed for the pencil skirts. I reasoned that a person shaped like a big pink eraser should not be harboring pencil skirts. Then, I realized how graceful they looked just hanging there. Their fabric far superior to the latest polyester or nylon ones. Those skirts had class. How could I give them the heave-ho? They had done nothing wrong. What did Stacy London know anyway? So, I stopped picking on the pencil skirts. I would delve into the hand-me-downs.

I shouldn't feel guilt for getting rid of hand-me-downs — should I? After all, the HMDs were free. I didn't have a monetary stake in their evacuation. One by one I examined my hand-me-down collection. Most of the stuff in the HMD collection was nicer than anything I'd ever buy myself. I usually limit my own shopping to things less than $10. It was a habit I learned in college and continued to find useful, especially during the holidays when clothes are considerably more expensive. My "I'm with Stupid" shirt came from a mall kiosk for $9; the red color is perfect for holidays. I finally pried two maternity shirts out of the HMD collection.

The next thing I saw was my collection of anything pink. I hate to admit it, but I went through a phase where I just bought things because they were pink. Pink makes me feel pretty and serene. After all, they paint the walls in institutions pink to soothe the inmates.

20

Unfortunately, my pink phase overlapped my Polo phase, and there were three pink Polos that needed a new home.

Jon Cryer wears Polo shirts on *Two and a Half Men*. I wonder if Jon Cryer and I wore the same size. Aren't Polo shirts a classic? Don't people pay extreme amounts of money for certain colors of Polos on e-bay? One shirt has a stain that looks like the Virgin Mary—surely it would sell. Maybe Jon Cryer would be interested. Better wait on the pink Polos.

How about the old Halloween costumes in the corner? Now that's a for sure charity item. I found a great Bride of Frankenstein dress I'd forgotten I had—oh, no that was my own wedding dress, should probably keep it. How about my pirate costume? I looked awesome in my pirate costume. People said I looked like Johnny Depp. No one suspected I was pregnant. Definitely must keep the pirate outfit.

Time for a new strategy. What if I were to get rid of everything my mother gave me? Stacy London would hate my mother. She never gave me anything that wasn't defective, purchased from a yard sale, or both. Yep, that's the ticket. Right there on the end was a dress made out of crushed velvet. Might have looked great at some time in history—the Paleolithic Period—but, that could definitely go.

One time my mother bought me underwear at a yard sale. There was a pair of lacy thong panties. I kept them just so I could tell the story about my mom giving me my first and only pair of thong underwear, and they were second hand. Next to the crushed velvet dress, was a snot-colored velour jogging suit. I think it came from my mother-in-law. It was a few sizes too large. I never knew if that was supposed to be a commentary on my weight or if my mother-in-law also had the $10 rule. Maybe that is just something never discussed in polite company.

Surely, I could get rid of something from my cowgirl collection. There was a time when I danced to Billy Ray Cyrus's "Achy Breaky Heart" and dated cowboys. Not the faux cowboys you might find on the dance floor of a kicker bar, but the real kind you would find on a horse. It wasn't the most tasteful period of my life as the heavy-duty jeans and long-sleeve, snap shirts with yokes would attest; however, it was a time when I owned a pair of pink cowboy boots. A couple of cowgirl shirts wouldn't be missed.

I used to wear slips. Good girls wore slips back when clothing covered up stuff. Now, clothing is something that makes going half-naked expensive. I should get rid of the slips. No one wears slips anymore, unless it's on a music video—so they can show off their tattoos. Not since Oprah decided that slips don't hide anything important have women worn slips.

What about those two very nice wool skirts from the 80s? Okay, now these are older than a decade. However, the skirts are very high quality. What if I re-classified them as vintage? Vintage clothing is definitely older than a decade, right? Stacy says you should never get rid of vintage stuff unless it goes to a vintage resale boutique. My mother says styles repeat every thirty years. I should hang on to the wool skirts for at least another ten years or until Stacy London drops by.

I'd culled only enough clothes to fill a plastic grocery bag and I was getting tired. Maybe closet cleaning should only be done after a nap . . . or a stiff drink?

Bob

The patio door was open for only a few seconds while I dropped our latest assortment of cans, bottles, and junk mail into the recycling bin. I saw it happen. A lone housefly zoomed inside, not five inches from my face.

He was larger than the average housefly, but smaller than a plane. I remember my grandmother saying that houseflies were bad news, "They spot your lampshades and curtains." I wasn't sure what "spotting" meant, but even as a kid, I was smart enough not to ask.

I hunted down the flyswatter. It had never been used before; most flying insects in our house were just bored to death within hours. However, this fly was different; he seemed to be on a mission. He flew with purpose. I took several mid-air swipes. He zoomed around my head—mocking my futile efforts. I waited for him to land. He only did so on the 10-foot ceiling or the fan on it. As soon as I put the swatter down, he would make a low pass near my face. Ignoring him was the only answer.

I washed dishes. He watched from the curtains. I did laundry; he went up and back down the stairs to the utility room. I took out the trash (his favorite chore) and he flew inside the empty trashcan. I finally gave up my efforts to kill him and named him "Bob." I had a great uncle Bob. He smelled funny and came to all family gatherings that involved sweet potatoes

Bob continued to be my constant companion. He buzzed my head early each morning, as I got out of bed. He waited for me to shower and learned that the sound of the microwave usually meant food. He loved the cat's litter box and hated the vacuum cleaner.

Since flies only live about a month, I knew my time with Bob was limited. Maybe he did too. Bob lived each and every day to the fullest. He explored the washing machine and barely escaped when I closed the lid. He was fascinated by the freezer's cold air and rode the ceiling fan blades for a slow spin whenever possible.

He became my personal stylist, "Bob, does this make my butt look big?" Silence—much more tact than my husband. He was the consummate friend.

One day when I was packing up some items for charity, Bob was particularly curious. He kept landing on the bubble wrap and crawling inside the old vases I was giving away. Then he was gone. I placed the items in a box. Bob was nowhere to be seen. He was prone to MIA disappearances. Maybe he was just napping on the light fixture, or in the garbage. Hours later, I loaded up the car to head to the Salvation Army. After dropping off the donation, I was sitting at a traffic light when Bob buzzed my head like a Scud missile. He seemed angry, like I'd abandoned him for another fly. The ride back to the house was quiet. I was getting the silent treatment.

I opened the garage door and drove in. He didn't even buzz my head when I opened the car door. Our relationship was forever changed. He was still Bob, but some of the enthusiasm had gone out of his fly-bys. He was quieter now, more reserved.

Then one morning, I left my coffee cup on the counter while I did some chores. I'd seen Bob earlier sitting on his favorite perch, the light fixture over the kitchen table. I puttered around, putting things away, hoping to organize myself awake. I went back to my coffee and took a sip. "Yuk, OMG. What did I just drink?" I swept my mouth with my tongue. I found Bob.

He always had liked the smell of coffee.

Remember the Alamo

"Get up! We have to go to the hospital!"

"What time is it?" my husband asks, squinting.

"It is 3:30, probably a good time to go to the emergency room on a Saturday morning."

"Are you still sick?"

"No, I just heard their coffee is good! Get up!" I insist.

"I thought you said it was a virus."

"Not anymore. WebMD says it is more likely Salmonella poisoning."

"Can't he go to the hospital with you?" my

husband says, rolling over. He recently retired from the military after 24 years as a Navy pilot. The stress of real life is getting to him. He stumbles out of bed.

We arrive at the hospital and the triage nurse escorts us to the treatment room immediately.

"Where's that coffee machine?" my husband grumbles, while I fuss with the gown. An indifferent nightshift nurse carelessly stabs me, draws blood, and then inserts the IV. Obviously, concern for my well-being is overwhelming my husband; he abandons me in his quest for caffeine.

In 18 years, except for the birth of our two children, I have never asked my husband to take me to the hospital. Each of those times, I had to agree we could drive through McDonald's on the way. When our first child was born, the nurse brought my husband in from the donut cart down the hall when I reached eight centimeters.

He finally returns with coffee. "What did the doctor say?" he asks, tipping the Styrofoam cup to his lips.

"He says they might know if it is food poisoning from the lab tests."

"You're going to be here all day. We'll be

lucky to get out by dinner. I'm going to go find some breakfast," he says, stalking off again.

When he returns, he tells me how excited he was that the hospital cafeteria had a bottle of Tapatío. A hot sauce aficionado, all eateries are ranked by their ability to set his tongue on fire. Blessedly, the physician comes back, confirms my diagnosis, and we are released by 7:30AM. We have prescriptions and doctor's orders that include fluids and bed rest.

Once we arrive home, my husband, fortified by two cups of coffee and a hearty breakfast, volunteers to have the prescriptions filled. I slog upstairs and crawl back into the musty warren that has replaced my tidy bedroom the last few days. My husband calls our luncheon companion at the suspect restaurant and confirms that he too is hangdog sick and worshipping at the porcelain throne.

When I accepted my husband's invitation for lunch with an old friend at our favorite Tex-Mex restaurant—The Armadillo—I had no idea I would end up sick in bed for a week. Mexican food, especially this restaurant's daily "Alamo Special" is one of the many things my husband and I enjoy together—along with Chinese, Thai, Texas Barbeque, Italian and just about any other fare. But we have been saving money, so eating out is a rare treat. And what a treat this is. I've become so weak that a trip to the bathroom feels like a ten-mile hike. I put on my pajamas, crawl into bed and glance at the plastic bucket that is my new best friend. I take a guilty comfort in knowing our lunch companion is sick also. Only my goat-intestine better-half escaped illness.

My husband is gone for what seems an eternity. I rest for the first time in days under the analgesic effects of the medication from the hospital. Just as I begin to doze, I hear the garage door open. Doors slam, papers rustle and my husband stomps upstairs. He presents the sack of medicine as if he has bagged a winter's worth of provisions just before the big storm. He removes four boxes of diarrhea medication.

"Why so many?" I ask.

"Different ones for different symptoms."

"How many different kinds of diarrhea are there? No—don't tell me. There are over 60 pills here."

"I didn't know how long you were going to be sick."

"Where are the antibiotics?"

"Oh!" he says, slapping his head, "I left them at the store. Beer was on sale and I got side tracked. Be right back."

He returns about 30 minutes later, pulls

the medications out of the bag, and begins to brief me on their use, side effects, and warnings. I'm impressed. He normally has the retention of a goldfish.

He brings me water and discusses my next medication. It's odd, him taking care of me.

I'm no better the next day. I had planned to take my son shopping, instead I send my husband on the 8th annual back-to-school ritual. This time-honored tradition begins with the prospective student suffering the ancient water torture technique known as showering, followed by a forced march through the department store. This year, Dad would step in and try to locate the only three pairs of size 18 slim, relaxed fit jeans in the county. Dad would go armed with a coupon good only "before noon" on the second day of the biggest two-day sale of the year. "Don't forget socks. They always come in handy when you get close to the minimum purchase required to use the coupon," I say. He assures me he has it under control. He takes our daughter along for a driving lesson. She has a learner's permit and is always up for a trip to the mall.

They are gone for several hours. I wake-up and panic. Calling my husband's cell, I hear fumbling with the phone. "Hi, is everything okay?" I ask.

"We're trying to check out now. This coupon thing is really hard."

"Socks, did you get socks?"

"Yes, but I was still short. I ended up getting a couple of T-shirts. All I have to do is pay and find our daughter. Then I'll be home."

Another hour goes by before I hear the garage door. I wake up to what sounds like buffalos in the hallway. Our son runs into my room very excited. "What is that smell?" he asks, putting on the brakes.

"Did you find some jeans?" I say.

"Yeah, look at these. And I got the coolest T-shirt ever. Feel it. It's sooo soft."

I look at the gray T-shirt. It has a picture of a martini and a cigar lying by its side. The logo on the shirt reads, "It's Happy Hour Somewhere." I'm taken aback. Who would buy a thirteen-year-old a shirt with a martini on it? The answer to my question walks into the room. "Why would you buy him this shirt?" I ask.

"We were in a hurry. We just had to find something to reach the coupon amount."

"What about socks?"

"I thought it was 'buy one, get one,' but it was 'buy one, get one half-price,' so we had to go to the higher coupon."

"So you bought a T-shirt with a martini on it?"

"It was all very confusing."

"More confusing than landing an aircraft on a ship in the middle of the ocean?" I knew I had him here.

He glares back at me as if I have violated national security. Back to school shopping is not for the faint of heart.

The next morning I'm greeted with improved intestinal health, but the days of illness have left me weak. It is my son's school orientation day. There is paperwork to be filled out. Information about emergencies is taken seriously by the school. I ask my husband to look at the forms. He takes one glance at the side written in Spanish and calls in our daughter for help. She turns the form over to the side written in English and hands it back. He is no better off. I know we are in trouble when he asks me how to spell our dog's name. He can't believe that the school needs four emergency phone numbers. He is not even aware that we have a pediatrician. Why wouldn't they just take our son to the emergency room, he wants to know. I have no answers. Mine is not to question the system, only to complete the paperwork.

My daughter comes in with concerns about my health. She wants to know when I will be better. I assure her it will be soon. She says she needs to go to the mall. She tells me that driving with her dad makes her nervous. I explain that driving with her father makes us all nervous. He sees driveways as "landing strips" and pedestrians as "bird hazards." She is not comforted. She wishes me well and heads off to shop online.

She returns about an hour later. "What size should I order these boots in?" she asks, just as I am dozing off. I think I'm hallucinating.

"What?" I say, looking fondly at the bucket.

"I like these boots," she says, turning her laptop towards me. "What size should I get?"

"I don't know. What sizes do they come in?"

"I don't know. Someone said they run large. Someone said they run small."

"See if they come in half-sizes."

"They don't. What do I do? Maybe Dad will know?"

"Yea, that's the ticket. Wait for Dad. He'll be able to hook you up." Sick for a few days and I have lost all credibility.

34

Later in the day, my husband comes in to check on me. "Can I get you anything?" he asks. "It's team night at Chili's." A portion of the proceeds are donated to my son's football program.

I glance at the bucket. Food could be good. I am thinking of my favorite high-fat, high-carb fare. My mind scans an imaginary Chili's menu.

"How about chicken noodle soup?" he says.

"Chicken noodle soup? What about Chili's?"

"You can't have Chili's. We're going to Chili's, you need something bland."

"How 'bout a malt?" I say.

"Number one, you are lactose intolerant. Number two, the antibiotic bottle says no dairy products." This from the man who can't use a coupon. It's wrong.

By the next day, laundry is starting to pile up. "Someone should put in a load of clothes," I say, as I step over the pile that has outgrown the closet and is spilling over into the hall.

"I'll have my daughter get right on it," my husband responds.

"She's not here. Remember, you took her

to the mall."

"Oh yeah, I'll have my son do it."

"You told him he could go to Zack and Riley's to play."

"Oh yeah."

"I have an idea. Why don't you put in a load?" He glares at me. "Just throw in some jeans. It'll be easy. I'll talk you through it."

"I know how to do laundry. I do laundry sometimes when I'm out of town."

"Then why do you always come home with a suitcase full of dirty clothes?"

"Because after the clean ones have been in the bag with the dirty ones, they are all guilty by association." This from a man who once admitted he slept on his sheets for six months without washing them. He half-heartedly picks his own clothes out of the ever-widening pile and heads downstairs to the laundry room. I retreat back to the musty warren.

Somehow, the household manages without my help. Meals are prepared, but sauerkraut is now served as fruit. Whole-kernel corn is a breakfast item. Bathing suits double as pajamas.

He plans a trip to the grocery store for milk and bread. I explain the markdown rack. Great deals from the bakery-deli can be found there. He likes the markdown rack. He comes home with four loaves of onion-dill bread. He serves it as toast with oatmeal. He tells me that our children are old enough to take care of themselves and points out that even pets that go feral learn to survive—that things are running so smoothly, as soon as I am well, I should look for a job. Ignoring the pile of clothes in the hall and the remaining loaves of onion bread in the kitchen, he begins to read me classified ads for jobs. I doze off just as he starts to recite the qualifications for a "landfill heavy equipment operator." Ah! Blessed sleep.

I wake from my nap. He informs me of his epiphany that if I find something part-time, I can continue to drive carpool. I inform him that he is spending too much time in the alternate universe known as "Facebook." He seems to be more aware of what his high-school friends are up to than his own children because he spends several hours a day reliving his glory days.

At one point, I get lost in the dirty clothes pile trying to find the bathroom. He is unable to hear my cries for help from the smelly pile of microscopic life crawling down the hallway and doesn't even look up from his computer when I disappear behind it. He is engrossed in a video of "the world's largest zit" his friend posted on Facebook.

He resumes his quest to find me the perfect job. I suggest that perhaps I should relocate to a better job market and he can stay behind and care for the children. He is appalled that I would suggest such a thing. "You would miss me!" he says adamantly.

"Not if I had a good scope." I retort. The gun enthusiast in him shoots me a sharp glance.

It is the first day of school. He wakes up our two teenagers and tells them to have cereal for breakfast. I mention other choices, like eggs or oatmeal: things that he likes for breakfast also; things that have to be cooked, because he will not eat cold cereal. He says not to worry about him. He will just go out for breakfast. I am concerned for his health—I may kill him.

I send him to the store. He is once again gone longer than it takes to purchase two gallons of milk. I am afraid he is buying more onion-dill bread. I should never have told him about the markdown rack. He finally comes home and tells me that I should clean out my car, evidently, someone has spilled the contents of my purse on the floorboard, and it's a mess. I thank him for the words of encouragement. His faith in my recovery is unfailing. He prepares me a slice of onion-dill toast before he goes to pick the children up from school. I'm just happy to have food that hasn't been recalled by the Center for Disease Control.

I continue to improve, but still have bouts of fever. I go to sleep burning up, only to awake shivering. My husband helps me pull the covers up. He dutifully finds the thermometer and checks my temperature. It is below normal. He gets back in bed and wraps his arms around me to stop the shivering. I finally drift off, feeling safe and warm.

I get out of bed and go downstairs. Someone has washed the dishes and wiped the counter off. I open the refrigerator with the intention of eating. Once the cold co-mingled smells of leftovers and vegetables invade my senses, I'm no longer hungry. I head back to bed.

My husband finds me and offers to fix me something. As tempting as the leftover buffet seems, I decline. "I'm hungry," I tell him. "However, the only thing that sounds remotely appetizing is chocolate."

"What kind of chocolate?"

"The kind with nuts in it."

"What kind of nuts?"

"Oh, cashews, peanuts, almonds—I'm not

picky."

"Medicinal chocolate it is! I'm on it," he says, leaving the room.

I figure I might not see him before Christmas, but he returns half an hour later. I hear him tell the kids the chocolate is only for mom. They complain, "We never have chocolate except on Halloween and then we have to dress-up and beg the neighbors."

"This chocolate is special. You can only get it in California with a prescription," I hear my husband say. The kids don't buy it. He stands his ground on medical reasons.

The chocolate tastes good, but not until I get to the chocolate covered cashews, do I realize it is the sodium I am actually craving. Somehow, this knowledge takes a lot of the chocolate satisfaction away. "Hey, would you mind getting me a pizza?" I ask my other half.

"Pizza. Why pizza?"

"Well I am pretty sure I need the salt."

"Couldn't I just bring you the salt shaker? Or a margarita?"

"As good as that sounds, I would settle for a frozen pizza." He returns to the kitchen and I hear the freezer door open.

"Cheese, pepperoni, or zucchini?" he yells

up the stairs.

"Zucchini?" I say, thinking I misunderstood him.

"Yeah, it was on sale, ten for $10."

"Don't tell me we have ten zucchini pizzas."

"O.K., I won't. But they are small."

"Zucchini it is."

My son comes in to check on my progress with the chocolate. He, too, informs me that someone has spilled the contents of my purse all over the floor of my car and credit cards, keys, and lipstick are everywhere. I thank him for his concern. I feel much better after eating the pizza.

The next morning, I feel a portion of my strength returning. It is a beautiful day and we drive to the zoo so I can have some fresh air. Our son and daughter retreat into their electronic cocoons, paying more attention to the miniature screens than the scenery. An hour later we arrive at the zoo, take a parking ticket and find a space. As we climb out, I tell my son to put on his shoes. He rifles the contents of the back seat and then confesses he did not bring them. A search of the car confirms this. We leave the parking lot in search of a 99 Cent Store and finally ask directions, locating one eight blocks away. The children are fascinated at the prospect of buying shoes for a dollar; everyone gets out for the adventure. Mesmerized by the variety of junk for sale, we scatter as if pulled by magnetic bar codes. The detour takes longer than anticipated. We leave with a Chinese finger trap and cheap flip-flops. Upon our return to the zoo, our son can't open the door; he's caught in the Chinese finger trap. We coach him out of it and proceed to the animals.

It is an enjoyable afternoon. The crowd is light and our offspring have never seen the zoo's hallmark, a crook- necked giraffe. It is good being together. My husband and I realize our own cubs will soon strike out on their own. They will go off to college and we'll be left with phone calls, tuition payments and the occasional lost sock. They are good children; we have been lucky. I wonder if it is too soon to throw away the Ace's Bail Bonds refrigerator magnet.

After a few hours at the zoo, we head home, hoping to beat the traffic. Approaching our neighborhood, we exit the freeway. At the first traffic light, my son looks up from his Game Boy and announces he is hungry. The rest of us agree. He points excitedly to a local restaurant and says, "Hey, remember The Alamo?!"

"As a matter of fact I do," I say, rubbing my still tender abdomen.

The lemonade diet

My husband is obsessed with his weight. He was a wrestler in high school and still has an adolescent addiction to the numbers on the scales. Sometimes, he weighs himself three times a day. I think he posts his weight on Facebook, in case his alma mater calls on him to show those youngins' how it's done. And he doesn't have an ordinary standard set of bathroom scales. His scales are programmable and track body fat just in case his Twinkie habit escapes the technological limitations of the digital weight feature. Other times he walks around with a bath towel wrapped around his waist and asks me if his belly looks big. I'd never say "yes." People should be able to walk around half-naked, in their own home, without feeling fat.

So, I shouldn't have been surprised when he wanted to go on the Lemonade Diet. For those of you who aren't familiar with the Lemonade Diet, it is ten days of consuming nothing but Lemonade, peppermint tea, and saltwater and is supposed to rid your body of any lingering toxins. It was developed by a doctor who wrote a handbook avowing its benefits.

Personally, I was just hoping to find the gummy bear I'd shoved up my nose when I was four.

A friend had been on the diet and reported weight loss of monumental proportions to his monumental proportion. However, I suspect that if you weigh over three hundred pounds, just picking the lemons might be the first step to improved health. But we already had lemons. Our neighbors had a lemon tree that dropped the football shaped fruits across our fence.

What did surprise me was when he asked me if I wanted to go on the diet with him. "It's a great cleanse," he said. "It's supposed to have a lot of health benefits."

I had been trying to lose the same five pounds for ten years and thanks to GPS technology and restaurant food they kept finding me. So, I agreed. After all, I'd been a teenage girl. I had lived for a month on cabbage soup and for weeks on grapefruit. I wasn't afraid of a few hunger pains. Then he explained to me that the lemonade has cayenne pepper and Grade B maple syrup in it. Now, I didn't even know what Grade B maple syrup was, and I couldn't even imagine a beverage that could be improved by cayenne pepper . . .

I pondered a few options: the blended watermelon daiquiris we made in college made with cayenne pepper instead of watermelon seeds ... no, probably not; the raw milk we had on our farm growing up with cayenne ... no way, not even after the cows had been eating wild onions; the bitter Russian vodka – straight from the freezer – I'd consumed with real Russians ... not hardly; the green tea served in some Japanese restaurants which tasted like it had been aged in the back of a toilet bowl ... No, there was nothing on the beverage menu that could be improved with cayenne pepper. But maybe, just maybe, the maple syrup would help ...

Then he told me that *lemonation* required power. The putsy little hand juicer I already had would never be adequate for the number of lemons that needed to be obliterated. I explained to him that the act of juicing by hand could be the secret to the weight loss – it might

46

be the calories burned in the juicing process that actually causes the pounds to disappear. I lost this argument; we were off to the stores.

Six hours and dozens of lemons later, we had lemon juice. It hadn't been an easy task. Some of the lemons were ultra juicy and shot all over the kitchen. Some of them had the consistency of a roll of paper towels. The pulp clogged the juicer's drain. Once a lemon became wet, it was hard to hold on to, and when it dried, it was as sticky as a Clinton love affair. It was not a job for wimps. We'd become a lemon juice manufacturer. By the time we got finished and cleaned everything up, we only had a gallon of lemon juice, an icky floor, and no fingerprints. Evidently, the acid in all those lemons also got rid of our ridges. I felt free in the knowledge that I could be an international jewel thief with no fingerprints to identify me.

My husband mixed up the magic elixir. When he added the cayenne, syrup, and water, it turned the color of urine. "Do you want a glass?" he offered.

"That's okay," I said, looking at the clear container. "I'll just wait until tomorrow when it has chilled." Then I went upstairs to update my will.

Surprisingly, the first day on the Lemonade Diet went exceptionally well. The lemonade had an earthy flavor with fruity undertones. I wasn't hungry at all. The liquid made the trek across my tongue and undiscriminating pallet on to my gullet with no problems.

On day two, the lemonade was a little woody and reminded me of a winter breakfast with tart pancakes. Again, I felt no hunger pains and had plenty of energy.

By day three, the lemonade began to taste a little boring. The cayenne no longer bothered me and the syrup was no longer sweet. I was proud of my determination. I hadn't even been tempted to eat real food. Bolstered by my new outlook, I decided to get on the scales.

"I've gained four pounds!" I shrieked, in my husband's direction.

"It's probably just fluid retention," he deadpanned. "I've actually lost five pounds."

"That's so wrong," I said, screaming.

"You probably just need to drink some of the saltwater. It's made with sea salt."

"Isn't salt supposed to make you retain fluids?"

"You should've read the book."

"I tried, it had no narrative drive, and the characters were flat."

"The salt ions bond with waste products and eliminate them. I'll do it with you. It works really fast," he said, ignoring my literary critique.

So, we drank a couple of quarts of salty water. My husband headed to the bathroom while I waited.

He returned to the kitchen. "Wow. My weight went down two more pounds," he said. "How do you feel?"

"Like I'm ready to audition at Sea World."

"You might need some more salty water," he says.

So, I drink another glass of the sweaty tasting liquid. Still nothing.

"Maybe you should just wait. I have to go back to the bathroom. I wonder how much weight I'll lose by tomorrow?" he said excitedly.

Frustrated, I decided to go to bed. I didn't want to know if he'd lost another pound ... or even another ounce.

By day four, the lemonade tasted like mulch, and I'd gained another two pounds. I had visions of eating salad with vegetables, dressing, and croutons. The thought of croutons made my mouth water. My husband, however, had lost eight pounds and was posting his new Facebook status as, "Now at my high school weight." Then we climbed our fence in order to make more lemonade. I was sure that lemon rustling was illegal. My husband was certain we were utilizing a natural food source.

Later, we were speeding down the freeway when I said, "I think we spent too much money on the juicer." He said he thought that $40 was reasonable.

"The juicer was $75," I countered.

"No, it was $39 plus tax. I should know. I paid."

"Bet me," I said.

"Okay, anything you want," he said.

"You make the next batch of lemonade by yourself," I said in a challenging tone.

"What about your career as an international jewel thief?"

"What about my increasing girth? How many international jewel thieves are fat?"

We exited the freeway, and drove toward the kitchen store where we bought the juicer. After we got out, I took the lead toward the storefront. I cherished my ability to remember prices. He was way out of his league ... my victory at the small appliance department was a small one. His brain was never designed for competitive shopping. It was like taking candy from a baby.

On day six, I was convinced that I might not ever get back into my spanks again. I felt bloated, tired, and never wanted to see another lemon. My husband said he felt great, like when he was in high school. I felt like turning myself into AARP.

"Let's go for a walk," he said. "Maybe you just need some exercise."

"Maybe I need to stop drinking a gallon of lemonade a day."

"I've lost 11 pounds. You must be cheating. Are you eating?"

"No, I haven't had a bite of food! A few sticks of gum maybe, and maybe a couple of bites of toothpaste, but I couldn't help myself ... it smelled so delicious, like cinnamon buns."

"That's the heightened sense of smell you get from the diet. Let's see if a walk will help. Maybe the four miles to the golf course and back?"

The first mile was good. We were just two people walking on a beautiful sunny day. By mile two, I was feeling tired. We stopped to drink water. The start of mile three, I noticed my husband was running into me on the turns.

A little later, he began stepping on my feet. My head ached and we stopped to rest. After the rest, we disagreed on which trail led home. We started down one path and bumped into each other, complaining like drunken rappers.

Some of the trails merged near our home, but not all of them. We argued about the trail but then we had to rest. We'd become a couple of lemonheads. Our IQs were dropping faster than Neilson ratings in July. We were less than a mile from our house and we couldn't go home. Someone needed to drop the hammer — it would be me.

"How about Mexican food?" I said.

"Mexican food! Don't you want to finish the diet?"

"No. I want to go home, get in my car, and go eat tortilla chips and guacamole. I want enchiladas. Can't you have cayenne pepper on enchiladas?"

"I'm hungry for fish tacos," he said.

"Fish tacos it is. No guacamole?"

"Definitely guacamole," he admitted.

We made it home in record time.

The walnut polish

My husband purchases spa days for various gifting occasions. This man, who reads the fine print on gum before he chews it, has never actually been inside a spa. However, he has no problem spending money over the phone on things like *The Body Bliss Package* and *The Stress Buster Facial and Massage*. While the saleswomen's voices may be sultry and efficient, my experience is that the spas themselves are usually disorganized dens of overpriced torture. Or perhaps it's just me. On that one day of the year, when I happen to have my appointment, the employees either have PMS or are celebrating National Bi-Polar Day. Whatever the case, I can't see myself surviving this trend much longer, which may explain why he wants to increase my life insurance.

My first spa experience was during Mardi Gras in New Orleans. It sounded like heaven. The day of pampering included a massage, pedicure, facial, and champagne lunch. All I had to do was get to the French Quarter while avoiding the parade route. Surely Map Quest did not intend for this to be done sober. I zig, I zag—barely missing two transvestites and a mime (I probably should've hit the mime).

I arrived at the spa, signed in, and then took my ultra-fluffy white robe to the assigned dressing room. Once they took my clothes away, the spa staff was nowhere to be found. I guess they thought I wasn't going far, dressed like a giant marshmallow. It would be a mistake, however, to underestimate clients during Mardi Gras. People have enjoyed many a parade dressed in much less.

Eventually, someone escorted me to a pedicure chair, which was similar to a dental chair with a bidet swirling at its foot. I sat there feeling like the Queen of the Whos waiting for the Cat in the Hat. A very nice lady sat in front of me, introduced herself, and began to eliminate my toes' cuticles. Ultimately, all ten toes were cuticley deprived. Then she began to eliminate my calluses. It started to hurt. Pain shot through my foot and up my leg. She was chatting to a co-worker in a language I didn't understand. They seemed to be deciding what to order for lunch. My teeth clenched. They decided against Chinese. My fists tightened. One of them had a coupon for Subway. Finally, my mouth opened in a silent scream. There was blood. The swirling water turned red! They decided on Italian.

"Oh, my goodness!" she said, as she removed the oozing pinky toe from the water and tried to stop the bleeding. "You have very sensitive skin." Ice was applied. How could people actually enjoy the aggressive sandpaper attacks?

She bandaged my foot and painted my toenails dark red from a bottle marked "Whiney Wine" without further incident.

I limped into the lounge and selected lunch from a menu. It arrived with champagne. I rarely drink and I've never had champagne with lunch. I was feeling very avant-garde despite the bandage on my foot. I had a second glass of champagne then it was time for the massage.

Naked and inebriated — not unusual for typical Mardi Gras revelers — I climbed upon the table. But I felt vulnerable. There were scented candles and soft music. I recalled a cheap date from college. The masseuse began to rub my back. "How far would you like me to go?" she asks. Again, it reminded me of a cheap date in college.

Diffidently, I replied, "You can go really deep." My face went numb when she rubbed my shoulders. I tried to speak, but no words came out. At some point, I blacked out from a sharp pain that started in my back and shot through my temples.

My next clear recollection was the masseuse helping me back into the fuzzy robe. The candles and music had been replaced by fluorescents and chatter. She took me into another room for the facial. My foot hurt; I limped. I climbed up on the new rack. The latest spa employee eyed me like fresh meat.

"What kinda fayshawl woodchew like?" she said. "I got abbacoddough, huneeamond, citruss mareange, whacheveryouwan."

She's a Cajun cannibal, I mused, offering marinades prior to the big feast. "I have sensitive skin," I said. "I'm prone to breakouts." "Moosherrizing fayshawl," she decides. I was relieved. This should be painless. For the next thirty minutes, she smeared on one lubricious concoction after another. "Diz juan revines," she told me. "Diz juan kleen dem pours," she said. "Dis juan mek you glo."

My cheeks began to sting. I was definitely glowing—red-hot! Eventually, I bid the voodoo priestess farewell and began searching for my clothes.

I limped to my car. I couldn't turn my head. By the time I got home, I was stiff and dizzy. My back ached, I was hung over from the champagne, and my face burned. Areas of raw skin on my forehead were oozing a clear liquid. I shuffled to the medicine cabinet and took an aspirin. My husband asked me how it was. "Great," I said, "I had champagne with lunch."

* * *

Not having learned my lesson the previous year, I called "The Sanctuary" and made an appointment for a pedicure—an online gift from my mother-in-law. I don't think she knew about my first spa experience, so I assume no malice was intended.

"We have moved recently," another sultry voice on the other end of the phone told me. I got directions from the voice.

Unfortunately, upon arrival, I found that the aging office complex was extensive and my sense of direction wasn't. I found the pole-dancing studio, the rock climbing gym, and the piercing parlor. I found the Forever Young Health Studio and finally, at the very end of the boardwalk, the recently relocated reprieve. I went in. There were scented candles and soft music — which made me wary. I gave them my name. They escorted me past Grecian statues and small fountains to a back room. I overheard the sultry voice on the phone.

The manicurist explained that the new pedicure chairs had not arrived, so she was using a portable pedicure unit and I'd be sitting on an old office chair. She also informed me that she "just fills in here occasionally," as she searched high and low for a way to fill the reservoir. "There should be a hose," she said. She settled for a pitcher and poured water into the strange square apparatus on wheels. I sat in the rickety chair and she rolled it over and put my feet inside. Then she realized we needed to relocate closer to the outlet.

I got out, stood on a towel, and scooted the chair and myself over to the outlet. She rolled the unit over, plugged it in, and turned it on. Loud groans were emitted: a cough, a belch. Then water spewed up to the ceiling like a sprinkler, drenching me from head to toe on its way down. "Oh, I guess I didn't get it completely full!" She laughed and handed me more towels.

Where the hell is the champagne? I'm having second thoughts about my mother-in-law's motives. Moisture continued to drip off the ceiling as she poured in more water and then massaged my feet. Finally, she commenced to make my toenails look more like art than thousands of years of evolution.

While I was sitting in the creaky office chair, drying off, a woman wandered in to introduce herself, and informed me that she was in charge of Botox injections, since this is a medical spa. (No, not an ordinary spa, but a *medical* spa!) She was frightening, with the sort of deep facial lines etched from decades of teeth clenching, snarling, and cigarette smoking. (I thought she should visit the *Forever Young Health Studio* next door.)

I wondered if my mother-in-law sent her. She seemed sincerely disappointed I didn't look wrinkled enough or perhaps lush enough for a Super Deluxe Botox Package deal. She grabbed a broom and left. I prayed that the flying monkeys would not be visiting me next.

My final spa experience involved "a gift certificate of monumental proportions," my husband assured me. "This is the Mecca of spas. A facial, manicure, pedicure, massage, and a Walnut Polish," are included in the gift certificate," he promised. I had finally arrived.

On the appointed day, like any princess, I drove my '92 Saturn to the royal palace of spas. Another sultry-voiced woman looked down from the Mt. Olympus reception desk as if I'd wandered in mistakenly, thinking it was a thrift store. "May I help you?" she condescended, over horn-rimmed reading glasses.

"I have an appointment."

"Perhaps, a hair appointment?" she queried in disbelief, pointing across the hall to the hair salon.

"No, a spa appointment," I said. I shouldn't have parked my car in front. Primer always makes a bad impression.

"Your name?" she probed dubiously, her voice losing some of its sultry quality. Finally, after conferring with her colleagues, she returns. "I need your gift certificate. They will be out for you in a moment." By then her voice had lost all of its sultry quality.

It takes more than one?

The girl came for me. "This way," she directed me down a dimly lit, exquisitely tiled hallway. She opened the door to the locker room and handed me a key. "You can take your clothes off and put them in here," she said, pointing to a locker. She handed me a paper thong and a fluffy robe. "You may step into the steam room until they come and get you, or you can have a seat in the lounge.

This left me with more questions than before: Who is *they*? Do I put the paper thong on for the steam room? Why can't I just wear the safe fluffy robe? On *Sex and the City*, they have towels in the steam room—don't they? Who else is in there? What are they wearing? If the thong gets wet, will it disintegrate? Was there a paper bra I missed?

I finally decided to have a seat in the lounge. Eventually, someone half my age walked in and mispronounced my name. "Right this way," she said, as I followed her into a dimly lit room with a large bathtub situated in the center. "Do you want warm water?"

"Yes. Very warm water," I said. She started running the water, took my robe and walked toward the door.

"I'll be back with the almond oil," she said.

"Wait, I thought I was getting my walnuts polished?"

"No, honey and almond," she said shortly, leaving the room.

I eased my shivering body into the tepid water. Where was the warm water I was promised? I turned the knobs. Damn, there is no warm water. I should've gone to the steam room. I curse again. The soggy paper thong rode up and I continued to shake, I couldn't wait for the almond oil girl to return. She never did. Finally, the cool, sticky bath was over. I retreated to the safety of the warm robe.

I was then moved to a smaller room with hot rocks for a massage. Scented candles were burning and soft music was playing. Another bad date, I thought. The stones, as they were called, stopped the shivering. I began to feel calm. The masseuse asked me what part I want her to concentrate on. Recalling the last painful massage, I opted for the legs. Given my prior experience, I figured if I could still feed myself afterward, I'd survive. I only cried out twice. How could such a small person have such strong hands?

I began to relax until I remembered the upcoming facial and pedicure. It'll be fine, I told myself. I'm at the spa of all spas: the *Holy Mother of spas*. The girl finished the massage. I slid off the table, I could barely stand, and my knees were trembling.

"I think you're finished," she said.

"Where do I go next? What about the facial, the manicure, and walnut polish?"

"I'll go check."

I stood there, shaking in the safety of the warm fluffy robe, and leaned on the table for support.

She returned. "That's it, you can get

dressed now."

I smiled, "Thank you," I said, taking a deep breath. I was saved. The sultry voice on Mt. Olympus must have been distracted. Maybe she lost her horn-rimmed glasses looking so far down her nose. I stumbled into the locker room, grabbed my familiar cotton underwear (they'd make a good grease rag when I was finished with them) and jeans. I tossed the wet thong into the trash.

Jogging down the long, exquisitely tiled hallway to the door, I fled potential unknown aesthetic procedures. I turned, smiled, and said, "Thank you," to the woman with the sultry voice as I passed. I jumped into my car and got on the freeway, checking my rear-view mirror frequently; no black-smocked women with sharp instruments could be discerned — they're not following me. My speedometer indicated I'd broken several land speed records, but I wasn't home. I needed a faster car!

Finally, I pulled into the safety of my driveway. As I was getting out of the car, my husband came out to meet me."How was the spa?"

"Great," I said. "It was great. But maybe next year you could spring for flannel pajamas."

Was prell "product"?

Do you remember the Prell shampoo girls? On commercials, they would lean over and flip their luscious locks over their heads and smile as the tresses cascaded back down to their shoulders when they straightened up. Prell was sexy and basic. Yet the Prell girls had every bit the hair the John Frieda and Paul Mitchell girls have for a tenth the price. And Prell didn't sell Prell Volumizer, Prell Gel, or Big Sexy Prell Hairspray. But, that was before we knew that sulfates—the ingredients in shampoo that actually clean hair—were carcinogenic and that we were no longer buying shampoo but "product."

The funny thing about most product is that it causes my hair to go flat along with my wallet. I wish I could just get a haircut and say, "I'll pay you extra to not use the word 'product' and not put any of it in my hair." But alas, no one would cut my hair because product is a huge source of income for most salons.

Sometimes I think hairdressers just like to use the word "product." It sounds professional. I remember when I thought "mousse" sounded professional. Now I know mousse is just another product that will force me to wash my hair the next day so I will be using more products to remove the other product, which hairstylists have gotta love. Before very long they have sold you an entire line of products that will work until the newer product comes along, which will be so much better than the old product, which is now known to cause cancer, eczema, or brain damage.

Funny thing though, I've never seen a class-action lawyer ad looking for plaintiffs to join a "product" lawsuit. Maybe product is exempt from the law like vitamins and supplements. Maybe product doesn't have to *do* anything or *be* accountable for anything. Maybe RJ Reynolds should reclassify cigarettes as product and save them a lot of money.

I remember a time before product, when there was money in *big hair*. Big hair was not possible without sulfates. People permed, teased, and sprayed to have big hair. We lived in the South and all my friends' moms had big hair. Big hair was as southern as Baptists and drive-thru liquor.

Women with big hair went to the hairdresser. Hairdressers knew everything. They were actually the first therapists. Women knew that no matter how bad life was going they could go see their hairdresser and come out feeling better.

I think a lot of the big hair happiness was actually the fumes from all of the chemicals that off-gassed from permanent wave solution and hair spray. Until this very day, I get a little kick from anything that reminds me of Aqua-net. It takes me back to a simpler time, a time before I knew that sitting at the hairdresser waiting for my mother to feel better was detrimental to my health.

My grandmother would wrap her big "hairdo" with toilet paper and then put on a hair net at night. As a kid, I thought this was strange and a little scary, but now that I have purchased product I am beginning to see the brilliance of it. How much money would I save if I used toilet paper and a hair net and only washed my hair once a week? Unfortunately, my husband would probably object. He still buys me gift cards for Victoria's Secret in the hope that they don't carry flannel.

My current hair stylist speaks English as a second language. Sometimes I agree to things I don't fully understand — which is how I end up with product. The last time she cut my hair, she asked me if I wanted bangs — I think. I came home with a tuft of hair in the middle of my forehead chopped off at a length that hung into my eye. I looked like a quail around mating season until I tamed it down with product.

I finally figured out that even if I don't buy product and I tip my hairstylist generously, she doesn't seem to mind my product phobia. She doesn't understand it — but like any good therapist, she keeps client confidentiality

My drawer of shame

Next to my bed is a nightstand. Inches from where I lay my head is the place where I keep secrets. It's where I put things I don't want anyone to know about. Useful things I can't seem to live without. Things that I cannot bear to part with; things I should've abandoned moons ago. Next to my bed is my drawer of shame.

I guess everyone has those items they don't know how to dispose of or can't bear to turn loose. Mine run on batteries. Batteries that were once vibrant and dependable are now dying from neglect. My drawer of shame is full of my old cell phones.

My husband forces me to replace my cell

phone when we change carriers. I find these transitions painful and clumsy. I should be able to use my cell phone with any carrier. I should be able to operate its every feature. I should be able to answer a phone call without hanging up on the caller.

Mindy, my first cell phone was the cute little flip one from '96. I could pull her out and flip her open in half-a-second. She was sleek and ergonomic, and fit comfortably between my ear and mouth. She folded up smaller than a pack of cigarettes. Since I don't smoke, I always had room for lip-gloss next to her in my purse pocket. Cute, sexy, ahead of her time ... then we changed carriers and my state of the art technology was replaced by the only phone our new carrier offered for less than the cost of a Coach purse.

Carl grew on me. He was about as sleek as a biscuit. He was dorky and awkward-feeling in my hand, but he had a genuine face. Simple, straightforward, Carl was dependable. What you saw was what you got — no fussy menus, no apps, and no wallpaper. Carl was the kind of phone your mother would approve of. He had an earbud for hands free conversing and he came with a car charger. Carl never did things without permission. The whole time I was with Carl, I never looked at another phone until one of those cell phone companies offered deep discounts. Then Carl was put out to pasture for unlimited minutes.

Veronica was my third phone. Not as cute as Mindy or as dependable as Carl, but she had class. No one who saw Veronica would mistake her for a burn phone. She was as high maintenance as a Jenny Craig spokesmodel. She had to have a new battery every ten months and fingerprints showed up on Veronica like thong underwear from the top row of bleachers. Eventually, Roni, as I affectionately called her, and I came to an understanding. I put her on the charger every night and she never died without whining first. It was a stalemate. She dictated demands like a diva and I acquiesced. I decided it was better than her dying without me. Life saving power stopped the moaning that caused strangers to look at me as if I was drowning puppies. Veronica was not a cell phone to be taken lightly, but she couldn't compete with Brandon's unlimited texting.

Brandon came with baggage. His box was smaller, but Brandon's extra-large instruction manual was written in five languages, none of them entirely English. Brandon could text. He had a slide-out keyboard, apps, calendars, a camera, and Bluetooth. Brandon had a rebate issued in the form of a gift card. Brandon was complex. His nuances were hidden underneath a sleek surface that belied his true talents. He seemed to have an unlimited power source. He could go all night...night after night. It wasn't until much later that I learned that Brandon's seemingly insatiable insomnia was due to his power saver mode, which sent most of my calls directly to voice mail. It was as if he didn't want me talking to my friends. Brandon was an enigma. He hid answers underneath menus. I had to tease everything out of him. Brandon's secrets were deep and dark. Unless I asked, he didn't tell me anything. Maybe he was the one. Ready to reject me in a heartbeat; Brandon peaked my curiosity. He played me like a free ring tone. I was ready to pay anything to keep his company. Surprisingly, Brandon and I are still together.

What am I supposed to do with my old phones? What if I go back to an old carrier? What if one night after too many margaritas (in a moment of weakness) I see the greatest deal in the world advertised by my ex phone company? What if I make that late night call and switch back to a former carrier? Wouldn't my old phone still work? Couldn't I avoid the whole "new phone awkwardness?" Is there anything better than going back to a comfortable, safe place where you know you belong? Where you won't be rejected because you accidentally pushed someone's buttons.

So, maybe my drawer of shame is really a place of comfort. Maybe there is a certain security in knowing that I can choose my own carrier. That no matter what sort of rate hike befalls my current phone company, I can take care of myself. That I'm not someone who can be taken for granted. Even Brandon should know that I refuse to be held hostage by initial offers and teaser rates. So, I'll keep my shameful dying phones and my antiquated technology. And one day when I least expect it, I might just make that call.

Hiking safety

I was surprised when my father-in-law said he was worried about my safety when I went on walks. I explained that the Conejo Valley, where we lived, has one of the lowest crime rates in the nation and I felt very safe. He opined that he wasn't just worried about the two-legged predators, but the four-legged ones as well. I reminded him that Conejo means "rabbit" in Spanish. On a good year, there are bunnies everywhere and even though they outnumbered me, I've never once felt threatened by one.

However, he was insistent that walking in the Santa Monica foothills could be a dangerous undertaking. So far, I hadn't even had so much as a tick bite, but I *was* a little intimidated by the mountain bikers who shared the mountain trail. The dodging and weaving to avoid them literally kept me on my toes and added an agility component to my workout. Bikers were a fairly passionate group. I could remember when I owned a bike; never once did I dress in spandex, declare myself king of the road, nor dare SUVs and garbage trucks to get in my way. I think all bikes should have those little bells to give the rest of us warning that some brightly colored maniac is about to use us like pins at a bowling alley. However, superheroes wear spandex, so maybe there is something empowering in it.

Was Dad suggesting I should do my walking in the mall? No, he said I needed "protection". I explained that I really didn't want a gun permit.

But, that wasn't what he had in mind. He had the perfect outdoor equalizer. He'd fashioned it just for me. He left the living room and came back with a large hickory axe handle almost as tall as I was. He had even drilled a hole in it for a leather strap.

"This is just the right weapon to take out a medium sized predator," he said.

I looked at the axe handle suspiciously. "It looks a little heavy." *It could take out a biker though.*

"I have others," he volunteered, running back to the garage.

After he presented me with a slightly smaller axe handle, I said "I think this should be just fine, especially, if a large male rabbit attacks." I left Dad feeling pretty proud of himself. *But why did he own an assortment of axe handles that even Lizzie Borden would admire?*

In the following weeks, I kept forgetting to take the axe handle with me when I walked. Finally, I made myself a quick note, "Remember the Axe", and stuck it on my front door. No one rang our doorbell for the next three days, not even Jehovah's Witnesses.

Finally, Monday came and I put on my Mickey Mouse sweatshirt, grabbed my Hello Kitty ball cap, filled my camelback (which was also a gift from Dad), picked up my axe handle, and waited for my walking partner. When she arrived, I confidently clipped on my fanny pack and my wrist weights.

"What's that," she said, eyeing my axe handle.

"For protection," I told her.

"Protection from what? Bears?" she inquired, ignoring Mickey and Hello Kitty.

"Of course not, I would've picked the larger one if it was for bears."

"It looks heavy," she said.

"It's not bad. Let's go before any of my neighbors see me and call the police."

The axe handle was a practical solution for hikers who didn't want to exercise with a baseball bat or an AK-47, but people still eyed it curiously as if I was headed for Disneyland, maybe to take a whack at Dumbo.

However, my parents-in-law kept insisting that they could improve my walks substantially with the proper gear. They love gear. Not just gear, but gear stores, gear magazines, and gear websites. Finally, they claimed to have found the perfect walker's companion—collapsible trekking poles. They had already purchased several pairs for themselves and were excited about the extra stability the poles offered. The next time I saw them, I came home with trekking poles.

One of the problems with the axe handle and the trekking poles was that a mile of my walk was in town next to a major street. I personally didn't care how ridiculous I looked in my own house, but venturing out with a Hello Kitty ball cap, a camelback, leg weights, and now, trekking poles, was pushing the envelope—even for me. The outfit alone was enough to discourage would-be attackers. However, the trekking poles worked great next to the sidewalk, but once I got onto the trail, it was a different story.

In the rocky Santa Monicas, the ground is defiantly hard. I tried to use the poles to steady myself on a steep eight-foot slope. I planted them just as I began the descent. About two steps down, the poles slipped and became flying projectiles while I landed on my back and rode the loose gravel to the bottom. Then I almost impaled myself when one pole became tangled on a nearby vine on the way down. I may not have looked death in the face, but I was at least getting a glimpse of its navel.

"Maybe I'm not using them right," I said at the bottom of the slope.

"Maybe you should put some marshmallows on 'em and build a campfire before you kill yourself," my hiking partner offered.

The next opportunity I had, I returned the trekking poles to Mom and Dad. "Thanks for the loan but I'm not coordinated enough to carry two things at once," I explained.

"Maybe you just need a single pole?" my husband interjected excitedly.

"Yes, I think that might be better," I offered politely. *What is with these people?*

The next day, my husband comes home

with a ten-foot piece of bamboo. "Look what I found for you!" he exclaimed. "It'll make a great hiking pole."

"Yes, I suppose it will. It's a little long though," I responded.

"I'll cut it off and put a leather grip on it.

"How many marshmallows do you think It'll skewer?" I had to know.

Rodent rescue

As I rounded the corner on my way home, I saw my teenage daughter's car parked next to the curb two blocks from our house. Out of gas, maybe? Check engine light? I continued up the street until I saw her walking and carrying her sweatshirt.

"Hey, what happened?" I asked, rolling down the window as I pulled up next to her.

"Mom, I found this squirrel. I wrapped it in my sweatshirt. It's paralyzed from the waist down," she said excitedly. "It's a boy; I'm going to call him Roger."

Injured squirrel, eh. I shouldn't be surprised. The child had brought home birds, mice, lizards, and bunnies — all in need of food, first aid, and time on my sofa. I come from a long line of animal lovers and so does my husband.

Our daughter seems to have gotten a double dose of furry-friend syndrome. Over the years, I've administered CPR to hamsters, knocked holes in walls to rescue wayward gerbils, attended fish funerals, and slept with many a puppy. Once, when my husband trapped a varmint in our attic and was coming down the stairs with the biggest rat I'd ever seen, my daughter yelled out, "We'll call him Norbert!"

I rolled up the window, continued home, pulled into my garage and waited. What I didn't need was an injured squirrel riding shotgun.

When my daughter arrived, we came up with a plan to place the squirrel in a box and make some calls to try and get him medical attention. If it was up to my daughter, she would have unlimited access to the local walk-in veterinary clinic and I'd be married to Bill Gates.

Somehow, during the squirrel wrangling and the cardboard rodeo, my daughter was bitten by the squirrel's end that was not paralyzed. We were still able to close the box with the squirrel inside, but decided to hold the lid down with a mop to prevent escape while we tended her wound and made phone calls.

The first call to the local animal shelter ended with frustration. I believe the woman's exact words were, "What-n-da-hell r you doin' wiffa hirt squirrel? Are you crazy? You go toda emergency room." Then she hung up. We went on the internet to search for proper injured squirrel protocol before making any more inquiries.

While we were researching "injured squirrels," my husband came home. His only concern was a box that had apparently fallen off the shelf and was blocking his parking space in the garage. The next thing I knew, a deranged voice was yelling my name— followed by several expletives—from the garage.

I raced down the stairs and into the garage to find blood everywhere. Evidently, someone had to shake the squirrel loose when it bit his finger after he reached for the box. Fortunately, the mop was now available for clean-up because SOMEONE took it off the cardboard box.

"I see you've met Roger," I volunteered to my wounded husband, who was standing next to the box holding the lid down while blood puddled on the floor. I returned the mop to the top of the box without speaking.

Then the phone rang, and my daughter ran to answer it (because that is what teenagers do). While I was explaining Roger's predicament to my husband, my daughter was speaking to someone from the animal shelter. Evidently, not all public servants are too busy to serve the public. I guess the animal shelter employee had overheard the previous phone call and called us back to give us the correct wild animal procedures for our area. It was one of many unheard of events in a very strange day.

The shelter woman said there was a local vet who did wildlife rescue for the county, and that rabies was not carried by squirrels in our area, but now we needed tetanus shots for the bites.

My daughter called me from the wildlife veterinary office. She was very happy, "Mom, they asked me if Roger could be returned to our neighborhood once he was better. I told them, 'yes!'"

I was so excited, all I could say was, "What-n-da-hell r we doin' wiffa hirt squirrel? Are we crazy?"

But it was too late. She'd already hung up.

Conejo chronicles

Conejo is the Spanish word for rabbit. But when I found out I was relocating to the Conejo Valley I wasn't worried. What's in a name? Los Angeles isn't over-run with Angels. Not until I realized that at least a dozen bunnies were living on my street, did I begin to get a clue. Finally, when my backyard began looking like an Easter Bunny convention, I understood how aptly named the area was. I didn't mind. I liked bunnies.

In college, I collected bunny-themed children's books with the excuse that they were for future offspring. Not long after that, the occasional stuffed rabbit would wonder into my dorm room and take up residence. I claimed homesickness and a love of anything small and furry as justification.

I continued to use this excuse as a young professional when I built a hutch to house a real rabbit. The Foo, named after the song "Little Bunny Foo Foo", lived in my extra bedroom and sunbathed on the patio. Meanwhile the stuffed rabbits had multiplied faster than real ones. When I married, my husband agreed to have children—probably hoping to relocate the 105 stuffed bunnies to a nursery.

So, when my T.O. neighbors pointed out that my dead grass was due to the bunny breakfast menu I served round the clock, I felt a little betrayed. In my first attempt to wean the bunnies from my grass, I planted Serbian bellflower in the flowerbeds for the bunnies' dining pleasure. In the parsley family, bellflower grows in bunches and blooms a beautiful purple flower. The bunnies loved it.

I felt so inspired by my eco-friendly solution, I finally read *Watership Down*. For two weeks, I was complacent in the knowledge that Hazel, Silver, and Fiver were smart and savvy enough to survive their forced relocation and, given a rabbit's inclination to procreate, they and their offspring would live happily ever after.

Then I was entering the garden center at

Home Depot when a young lapin cut me off racing for the vegetable plant six-packs on the floor. He threw me a knowing glance, tilting his long ears with a nod of his head and indicating he was allowing me to pass. I was still naively complacent in the knowledge that I lived some place where bunnies were welcome, even in Home Depot, and we could exist in harmony with the environment.

I would garden and the rabbits, unafraid, would still visit. I would weed and plant, they would nibble and chew. It was a perfect relationship — until I tried to replant my grass.

The garden center sold me ten pounds of grass seed, assuring me that germination was certain, sprouting was eminent and manure was in my future. The bunnies, however, had another plan.

There must be something irresistible about young innocent grasslings. No amount of Serbian bellflower was more tempting than the fresh seedlings trying to follow the straight and narrow path to becoming blades of fescue. The bunnies swooped in, chewing them off faster than a teenager can text. I think they send out the food critic who reports back to the consumption committee who informs the general who commands the sergeants who rallies all the troops to the mess hall.

If it hadn't been for the decision to sell my house, I would have lived happily ever after. But home buyers like grass. They like to think they can move in without worrying about things like dead lawns, leaky toilets, and pink flamingos. I set out to dissuade my long-eared guests from the bunny brunches and the rabbit repast.

My garden center guru said that rabbits don't like pepper. That sounded easy enough. So, I head to the store to supersize my pepper supply. Two pounds of coarse black pepper and 32 sneezes later, I was still entertaining the rabbits with my gardening skills. I returned to the nursery where I was told to try cayenne pepper instead. I dutifully bought and sprinkled enough red pepper to spark a rebellion in parts of Central America. Again, I was visited by a band of bunnies dedicated to the destruction of my fescue. I suspect their Mexican ancestors have made them impervious to the hot spicy condiment.

I decided to change gurus. I went to the hardware store and looked for someone named Mr. McGregor. I finally found a Mr. McGregor lookalike in the garden department who advised me to use a liquid product and spray it around the perimeter — guaranteed to keep out deer, rabbits and coyotes. I was immediately suspicious, because if I had a coyote in my backyard the rabbits would not be a problem. I purchased it anyway. As I sprayed the area around my wrought iron fence, I think I heard small noises in the bushes that sounded like tittering. My suspicions were confirmed soon after when I noticed the scout rabbit giving the all-clear sign to the others.

Now, I was hotter than the cayenne peppers sprouting in my backyard. This called for some drastic action. I went on the internet! I immediately found a guaranteed, 100% organic solution. For only $19.95 plus shipping and handling, I would be bunny-free in six-weeks. No, I didn't order a pellet gun, but garlic pellets. I waited in anticipation for the Fed-Ex delivery that would put me one-step closer to a sure sale in a bad economy.

When the big day finally arrived, I tore open the box and read the directions like a lottery winner with a mega-million ticket. It was straightforward and I was excited about the upcoming victory. I went right to work, scattering the bunny repellent pellets all over the yard.

I woke up early the next morning and peered out the window. The little four-footed terrorists were hopping about and munching down like bulimic teens at an all-you-can-eat pizza buffet. However, I was prepared for this. The directions encouraged re-treating the area at two-week intervals. Slow and steady wins the race. I continued my tortoise-like pursuit. But after eight weeks, the bunnies were still as regular as fiber commercials. The rabbits must have be Sicilian or Italian because the garlic only seemed to be drawing more of them and I thought I heard one of them refer to the lead rabbit as "The Don." I returned to the garden center losing my patience and my sanity. The guru told me my only choice is to install a small animal fence. No hole can be larger than an inch and a quarter. I tell my husband, who complains that we already have a very nice fence. I even consult my computer repairman, who handles all of my big problems. He recommends artificial turf.

We went to the hardware store to shop for rabbit proof fencing. The fence guy recommended artificial turf. We are undaunted — chicken wire will save us. We go to the lawn and garden department for more grass seed. The master gardener recommends artificial turf. We draft our children into our chain-gang fencing crew. We teach them the ends and outs of zippy-tie construction and secure the cheap wire fencing material to the expensive wrought iron existing one. Then we waited. I saw The Don scouting the fence line. He made several passes back and forth and finally left. We have a winner! I was so excited

I sowed the new grass seed in one session. This was going to happen—I could feel it.

The next morning I woke up to Hazel & Co. once again. I was as pissed as a Kardashian with a chipped acrylic. I walked the fence line while my nose ran from the smell of garlic and I sneezed from the whiffs of pepper. I finally found a fresh hole dug underneath the new fencing. "Rocks," my husband said. "We need a solid layer of landscaping stones; so if they dig the stones will block their path." Off to the hardware store again.

We were quietly discussing the barricade potential of various landscaping stones. I voted for the shorter paver-like ones. If a bunny burrowed under one of them, it would be more likely to fall down and block the tunnel. My husband is appalled at the cost. He voted that we drive to the desert and collect our own rocks. "Who would pay $1 a rock to keep bunnies out?" The salesman came by and recommended artificial turf once again. We look at each other and begin loading the stones into our cart. However, the next time I saw the artificial turf commercial on television, I wrote down the phone number—just in case.

Vittles for visitors

Over the course of one summer, we had seven different crews of friends and relatives come and visit—all welcome, all invited. I cleaned my house, watered my lawn, washed my car, and had my carpeting shampooed. After all, I really didn't want anyone to know how we really lived. What I didn't know how to deal with were the dietary idiosyncrasies of all of these people.

I'd grown up eating everything. Food pickiness was not something tolerated in my parents' home. When I was a kid, if I turned my nose up at a food, it was a sure thing I would be eating it for breakfast the next morning, and lunch, and maybe dinner. I even learned to love lentils

However, I have allowed my own children a little more latitude, but not that much. My son tried vomiting up food he didn't like. It took us an hour one night, to get him to try a spinach leaf and what followed was not something you'll ever see on Rachael Ray. Even this didn't keep us from requiring him to at least taste everything we served, but it did ruin a few meals for anyone else at the table.

For example, my 13-year-old football-playing nephew only eats grapes and things he can put ketchup on. Now, you would think that he would eat spaghetti because isn't the sauce kinda like ketchup? But no—meat, French fries and grapes—that's it. However, ketchup on grapes was also a no-no. In my parent's home, he would have found himself eating Brussels sprouts and oatmeal for breakfast and if he persisted—oatmeal, Brussels sprouts, and a peanut butter and jelly sandwich for lunch.

My brother, Eric, claims that he doesn't eat salad; that he is strictly a carnivore. I do recall him eating green beans for breakfast after one harrowing dinner when we were kids. Even when I tried to feed him my special salad with grilled chicken, he scoffed. However, I noticed when we went out to eat he ordered a salad. Evidently, it was just my salad he wouldn't eat. I was ready to stuff my special grilled chicken salad between two pieces of toast for his breakfast.

Jerry, my flexitarian brother-in-law, will eat fish, sometimes chicken, but no other animal products. I don't know if he is worried about the intelligence of cattle and pigs, or his own health. He doesn't drink milk or eat eggs. I guess somehow that the eggs carry more stigma than the actual chicken. I have to wonder how chickens feel about egg discrimination. He will however scarf on salad, which I deeply appreciate. Fortunately, my brother and my brother-in- law did not visit at the same time. However, my in-laws did come at the same time as their son, Jerry.

Now, my mother-in-law, Linda, doesn't eat fish, and she even refused to allow the use of her ice chest for fish products. Fortunately, we had leftover steak from my brother's visit to offer my mother-in-law. However, when we grilled outside, Jerry was worried about his fish becoming contaminated by his mother's steak on the grill so special precautions had to be taken.

Jerry decided to do the actual cooking and asked me if I had any hazmat suits. Since my husband usually grills in his swim trunks with his shirt off and yells, "fire" every time he gets popped by grease, I didn't think we had anything that would qualify as a force field against T-bones except an old Halloween costume, and my brother-in-law was against grilling dressed as a Jedi warrior. However, it turned out to be an excellent meal in spite of the cross contamination issue.

My niece, Alexandria, has a recognized medical condition and can't eat gluten. My sister-in-law has to prepare her food separately and take it along when they go anywhere. However, my niece can and does eat bacon, which is more than I can say for my brother-in-law, Jerry, who is her father.

God bless my father-in-law who will eat almost anything that doesn't eat him first, but he has sworn off regular soda. Now, both of my parents-in-law have a diet soda addiction. Diet soda is the bond that keeps them together. This common ally allows their palates to continue dining in the same restaurants. Unfortunately, it has eroded their taste buds to the point they can eat anything, anywhere, anytime—except fish, of course.

To spice things up even more, some of our guests preferred organic food. Now, while I don't have anything against organic food except the extra cost, not every food is readily available in the organic form. Therefore, I've come to think of pesticides and fertilizer as just another food group. However, I went on an organic-quest. I looked for foods that were pesticide free, fertilize free, antibiotic free, and hormone free. It was amazing how expensive the "free" foods were. I sought out the genetically un-modified, the un-irradiated, the un-processed, the un-chemically ripened, and the un-washed. I was searching for dirty, small, dark food that was as natural as a European armpit. I finally found organic coffee, organic wine, organic tomatoes, hormone free chicken and beef, and natural beer and ginger ale. What I didn't find was organic bacon. Someday, I hope to find organic bacon on Michelle Obama's *My Plate* — maybe a nice BLT instead of vegetables, grains, and proteins.

One guest objected to the brand of dog food we fed our Pug. She believes that dogs, being carnivores, should only be fed raw meat. Now, once again, I have nothing against raw meat, but the idea that I should be buying T-bones for my dog — while I eat lentils is a little disturbing. It already bothers me that my husband greets the dog first when he comes home. The fact that the dog would be eating better than me was like asking strangers to use the bathroom stall before I was willing to go in — it's just wrong. I put my foot down; our dog would have to eat dog food or leftover lentils.

While, I was never sure that all my guests were completely satisfied at every meal, I didn't have to force-feed anyone leftovers for breakfast.

Hiking with Mary

In the beginning, the six-mile hike was just a good walk. Then, it was a way to meet Labrador retrievers. Eventually, it became our spiritual retreat and walking shoe testing ground. Now, it's a way of life and we feel fortunate to live close to the Santa Monica Mountains. Its natural foothills lead us off the beaten path and into a place devoid of cars and pavement.

Mary and I typically begin walking when school starts in the fall after that big deep breath mothers take when all their children climb out of the car and become someone else's responsibility for six hours.

Several months into our first year, I spotted a beautiful buck on the path about fifty feet in front of us. He was large and looked straight at me with dark brown eyes. I froze and tapped Mary on the shoulder so she too could enjoy the miraculous brush with nature.

Mary, however, sensed danger, jumped up on my back, and began screaming and clawing at the air like a catnip-crazed feline. If there was any wildlife in the entire area, now they were long gone. Especially, after I collapsed under her in raucous laughter.

"Was it a bobcat?" she said, her dark eyes wide open with fear.

It took a second for me to get control of my bladder and pick myself up. I was having a hard time catching my breath after the bout of hee-haw.

"No, it was just a deer," I finally replied dryly.

"You're supposed to make yourself look big and fierce in case of mountain lions!" Mary explained.

"Well, at least I know who is going to be on top," I retorted still trying to compose myself.

Six months later, we saw a coyote meandering down our path. I braced myself for the wild-animal-piggyback. However, to my surprise, Mary simply confessed that she did not know what to do when a vicious coyote was pressing down on you. I was a little relieved at this and let my guard down some.

"Let's just keep walking, maybe he will be intimidated by our colorful New Balance walking shoes and just leave," I suggested. Mary eyed me skeptically and we kept going.

One day, we spotted a groundhog perched on a log. Excited, Mary and I crept toward it, holding our breaths. We had never seen a groundhog on our walks before. Just as we anticipated it would flee, we realized that its lethargic demeanor was a piece of driftwood lodged on a trunk. Needless to say, it didn't move at all.

There is also a huge assortment of lizards who sun themselves along our route. Some of them scurry off as we walk by. Others ignore our intrusion. A few budge only enough to hide their bodies under the brush, but leave their tails exposed on the path. One warm day, we came upon a tail sticking out.

"Oh, look," Mary said.

"Don't panic, but that's a snake—just a small one," I warned.

"Maybe it'll see our colorful New Balances

and just go away," Mary responded.

I look at her and shake my head. "Let's just walk over this way," I say, giving the reptile a wide berth.

"I'm glad that's over," Mary said.

"So am I," I responded, while Mary was climbing down from my back.

The great colon caper

The big 5-0 was not like turning 13, nor was it like my 16th birthday, or my 30th. It was better. My husband bought me a diamond ring and took me to Las Vegas for a surprise weekend. Friends met us there and we all went to Cirque du Soleil. I also learned an important lesson: the only thing better than a pedicure and manicure is a pedicure and a manicure while drinking a mojito. I left Sin City certain I could still enroll in one of those pole-dancing classes without missing a beat. Life was good.

Well, pretty good ... until I went in for my annual physical. My doctor said that since I'd turned fifty, I needed a colonoscopy. I couldn't think of anything involving the word "colon" that sounded even half as fun as a root canal. I assured him that I'd have it done as soon as they served alcohol during the procedure. What would he know? I wouldn't see him for at least a year.

And what a busy year it was. As the mother of teenagers, there were driving lessons, proms, and college entrance exams. There was turkey, a Christmas tree and what might be the last Easter egg hunt, I couldn't be bothered by anything involving the word colon. Then the reminder card about my next annual check-up came. I'd almost forgotten about my colon, except when I ate Indian food. I finally promised my check-up reminder card I'd call about the colonoscopy so I could see my doctor with a clear conscience. Another month went by before I began colon reconnaissance.

After seven phone calls, I learned that colon peeping is not a simple task. It would involve at least three appointments: an initial consult, the procedure, and the post procedure consult. Many gastroenterologists perform the procedure at a hospital. So not only would I have to find a new doctor, but navigate a new hospital as well. I finally went on the internet for more colon intel and eventually found a gastroenterologist that performed the procedure at a center next to his regular office, not far from my home.

On my first appointment, I sat down with the gastro guy. He explained the basics of the endoscopic examination of my colon using a small camera on a flexible tube inserted into my rectum. I envisioned a Rotor Rooter technician without the truck. Then I found out that my conscience wasn't the only thing I was clearing. The day before the colonoscopy, I would drink a gallon of liquid to flush out my system—something like Liquid Drano. Then on the day of the procedure, I'd check in to the surgical facility in the morning and plan to be there for two to three hours. They would be sedating me, so someone would need to pick me up after the procedure. He made it sound too easy. I was immediately suspicious.

"Do I have to be sedated? They do colonoscopies in Norway without sedation," I said.

"Why would you want someone to stick a tube up your rectum without sedation?" the doctor asked, incredulous.

"Why would I want someone to ram a tube up my rectum *with* sedation?" I countered.

"Good point," he acquiesced. "But what do you have against sedation?

"Isn't it the most dangerous part of the procedure?" I queried.

"No. The most dangerous part of the procedure is navigating the colon. There is a one in 3,500 chance of perforation. Out of those, only one in 30,000 are fatal. Sedation just makes the procedure more comfortable.

"Well, there is just no end to the fun," I said, pun intended.

"We fill the colon with air so we can navigate. It's the inflation that can trigger discomfort," he said. "If we find anything suspicious we will take a biopsy. Any polyps smaller than a millimeter we remove."

Now, I was really getting nervous—my colon inflated like an inner tube. I could see my Macy Parade balloon-self floating over the table with nurses struggling with tethers to keep me from floating away.

"What kind of anesthesia do you use?" I asked, wondering if there was any of Michael Jackson's dream juice involved.

"Usually, fentanyl and midazolam."

"It won't make me sick, will it? When my daughter was born, I threw-up on my husband as soon as the epidural hit," I volunteered.

"It won't make you sick. Anyway, you can't eat after midnight."

My last meal ... I pondered. What would I choose? Escargot? Steak and lobster? Maybe something horrendously spicy that would put me in Guinness World Records under the parade float category.

He escorted me to the nurse's desk where my last meal fantasy was burst when I found out that I would be on a clear liquid diet of Jell-O and juice the day before the procedure. But nothing red. The dye interferes with the resolution. If only there were black licorice Jell-O, I thought ...

The nurse gave me a prescription for the "Drano," an appointment card and I was on my way.

Since I was scheduled for the procedure in just two days, I went straight to the pharmacy where I received a plastic gallon container with powder in the bottom. Then I was instructed to fill the jug with water and start drinking the mixture a day prior to the procedure — eight ounces every fifteen minutes until all the fluid was gone. The pharmacist said, "I hope everything comes out okay." I didn't know if she intended the pun.

The Drano label instructions said, "Do not sip or drink it all at once." I considered adding rum and ice and putting it in the blender, but the next instruction said, "Do not serve with ice or mix with alcohol." My last meal would consist of something that looked like it was collected from a tire swing several days after a rain.

Once I began to drink the Drano juice, my stomach began to rumble. Noises resembling pterodactyl cries could be heard all over the house. I couldn't leave the toilet for more time than it took to drink the eight ounces. Three hours later, I decided it was more efficient to bring the Drano into the bathroom. My colon had effectively hijacked my life.

My colon continued its hostile takeover throughout the night. I used bedding to dampen the noise and relied on the bathroom fan for company. By morning, I had changed religions three times and forced our dog to take a vow of silence. I tried to apply a little make-up while perched on the white porcelain vanity seat. The lighting was bad — one in 30,000 chance I'd arrive in the morgue looking like a transvestite.

My husband drove me to the surgical center and signed a promise, which said he would return for me in at least two hours. After the notary was finished, I assured my husband the whole thing was covered in our prenup and he was obligated to pick me up.

A nurse took my blood pressure, heart rate, and temperature. Another nurse placed an IV in my arm. Then they took me into the room where the procedure would take place. The doctor came in and held my hand while he explained the wide screen monitor and the equipment. I really can't tell you what happened afterward. The medication has a sort of amnesic effect — like what happens when my mother starts talking.

The next thing I remember, I was getting dressed. They told me everything was normal, and my husband was picking me up. Then it gets a little fuzzy again. I remember he asked me if I felt like going to Kohl's because he had some shopping to do. Then I remember waking up in my bedroom. I felt fine. No pain, no need to visit my bathroom fan, and no strange noises. In fact, it was remarkably quiet. Then I saw a ladies' shirt hanging on my chest-of-drawers. "Hey, what's that?" I asked my husband.

"It's a shirt. You just bought it at Kohl's," he said.

"It's cute. I hope I didn't pay too much," I said.

"You got a really good deal."

"Did I have a coupon?"

"Twenty percent off. You used it," he said.

"So, how much did I pay?"

"Like three dollars. It was a steal."

"Wow, I can't wait until my next colonoscopy. Maybe you could take me to Nordstrom's afterward."

"It's a date," he said.

Exhausted from the shopping, I fell asleep for the rest of the afternoon. I think. I just hope I didn't enroll in a pole-dancing class.

The pug, the button, the insanity

Pugs are very smart dogs. Our dog, Pugsley, was no exception. He learned to sit, stay, and defiantly shake his head, all in record time. He was too smart for crate training, but he also seemed to think that relieving himself on our wool Oriental rug made him far superior to the cat.

Since we were condo dwellers, Pugsley didn't have a traditional fenced backyard and doggie door. We had to escort him outside to do his business. It finally occurred to me that, since our condo was large, maybe Pugsley just needed a way to signal us when he needed to be taken out. Hence, I invented *the wireless doorbell doggie doo-doo system*—the **W3D**. The system consisted of three parts: 1) A wireless doorbell button placed next to the backdoor he uses; 2) its chiming counterpart on the stair landing, which would alert everyone that Pugsley needed to go out; 3) and dog training lessons to teach Pugsley to push the button.

It took a few training sessions for Pugsley to learn to ring the bell. We started by pushing his paw down on the button before escorting him to the backyard. When this seemed to be going a little slow, we conducted intense sessions that involved button pushing followed by treats. Spurred by the extra incentive, he quickly learned to press the doorbell on his own and we continued to reward him with treats after a successful trip to the back yard. But after those first visits, things went awry.

In no time at all, Pugsley had our entire family trained. He rang the bell, and someone promptly came downstairs and opened the door for him. He would walk outside, sniff the flowers, bite a snail or a rock, and come back in for a treat. We quickly realized we were being used. Every few minutes he was pushing the bell. So, we decided to *only reward him only if pooped or peed.*

Once again, Pugsley was way ahead of us. He learned to control his bladder for maximum treat procurement. He would go out, barely squirt the grass, and then come right back in. As soon as we had returned to whatever we were doing, the chimes would sound again. He could get ten treats out of a full bladder and the added exercise was beginning to wear on us. If we tried to discourage him from going outside, he would casually walk over to the newly steam-cleaned Oriental rug and sit down, sniffing areas that he had "used" in the past. It was a threat! We recognized his curly, black tail techniques. We were playing a high-stakes game with sweaty palms; he was on to us immediately.

Eventually, we realized that bell ringing behavior increased around feeding time. He would go from a barely touched food bowl to the doorbell. Clearly, treats were tastier than his regular fare.

Back to the crate he went. We were not going to be out-maneuvered by 13 lbs of man's best friend. But in no time, he leveraged his way out of a $90 kennel. What had once held a wily, 55-pound boxer on a 2500-mile trip was mere child's play for the determined pug. By repeatedly jumping against the metal door, he loosened its welds. Then he ripped all the stuffing out of the dog bed until the entire kennel was consumed in gray fuzz. His romping and gyrating had also loosened the outer bolts that held the two kennel halves together. In a moment of weakness, we discussed getting him a small, flat panel television.

Finally, after the twenty minutes recommended by *Crate Training for Dummies*, we freed him from the cruel and unusual to escort him to the potty area. He ran through the house at full speed with ears flapping in the wind only stopping briefly to ring the bell. We'd been beaten by a master manipulator.

The fundraiser

I was surprised when my conservative husband expressed an interest in yoga classes. I was even more amazed when he invited me to a fundraiser for a homeless shelter sponsored by the yoga studio he frequents.

"There'll be music and dessert," he said in an enthusiastic Billy Mays' voice.

Rarely do I pass up a music concert and I don't think I've ever passed up dessert. So the answer was simple. "Sure, I'll go to your yoga thing. After all you did go to the opera with me."

"That's right! An entire evening of screaming followed by a tragic death," he said.

"You owe me."

"It wasn't screaming, it was singing," I countered with a better Billy Mays' impersonation.

"It was in Italian. It may have been screaming. We really can't say," he said.

"And all operas end in tragic death. It's the definition of opera."

"Why would you want to go if you already know how it ends?"

Comedian Jeff Foxworthy's tag line, "You might be a redneck if…" went through my mind, but I kept it to myself.

The fundraiser was held in a new age church. We arrived early enough to get chairs along with a couple dozen other people. Everyone else sat on yoga mats on the floor. The lights were low. There were candles, various instruments set up for the band, and tasteful contemporary art hung against purple walls. The smell of incense floated around. I was pretty comfortable until the church's minister was introduced in order to thank her for the use of the sanctuary. She was dressed in a purple pantsuit, and had on purple lipstick — neither of which bothered me — it was her purple hair that got my attention. Raised as a Southern Baptist, our ministers didn't even wear purple ties. I can't even imagine our Pastor Jim at the pulpit with purple hair. If I had, it would've been because I wasn't paying attention and I would have prayed for forgiveness right there on the spot. The only purple in our church was the grape juice used for communion because everyone knows that Jesus didn't really drink wine.

The barefooted owner of the yoga studio spoke and introduced all the instructors. Then some dedicated students received special recognition. The director of the shelter told us about its many programs. A man who had gone through the rehabilitation program spoke — overall, a very inspiring event. Then it was time for the musical entertainment.

The ensemble's singer had a tattoo of some ancient symbol on her arm and wore a skimpy lace-up mesh dress and bells around her ankle. She talked about God as her inspiration and I remembered when I wanted a bikini and my parents told me that God probably wouldn't approve. I figured God had become a lot more liberal than in my parents' day. My husband looked at me and raised his eyebrows as if to say, "Our yoga classes are not like this."

A drummer and a guitarist accompanied the singer. The drummer looked like he was straight out of a Dickens' novel. I couldn't keep my eyes off him. I expected the Ghost of Christmas Future to materialize at any minute. The guitarist looked more like he belonged in a country band. I kept trying to see if he had a Skoal can in his pocket. But once the singing started, I forgot all about the musicians.

Yes, those soprano mantras and Sanskrit prayers kept my rapt attention. The singer had all the passion of a cat in heat on a hot August night. It was a lot like opera, but without the pageantry, costumes, plot, and intermission. I was sure the First Baptist Church congregation would have pulled the fire alarm and thrown a blanket over her by the second song.

Then the people who were sitting on the floor stood and started dancing. A burst of insight leads me to an epiphany: why had the Southern Baptist religion condemned dancing early on? Because there are just some things white people shouldn't do.

They jumped, swayed, and rolled their eyes to the back of their head. It was like Woodstock, but without the excuse of rhythm and marijuana. After several minutes of dancing, the whole place started to smell like feet—incense and feet. I suppose that it was a perfectly natural smell— organic, even—but if I wanted to be around the smell of sweaty people in the dark, I would've gone to an orgy.

I leaned over to my husband and whispered in his ear, "You owe me so much opera. And I mean Italian opera, none of that Gilbert and Sullivan stuff."

"You're never going to let me forget this are you?" he whispered back, shaking his head.

"Nope. I've been wanting to see *Aida.* Thank you for making it happen."

"No problem."

I spent the rest of the event shopping for tickets on my iPhone.

Raising chinchillas

I love giving gifts. I don't know why, but it's one of my favorite things. So, when I saw the opportunity to give my husband's parents a gift that would keep on giving, I took advantage of it. After all, they had always been generous to me—one Christmas I received both an exercise ball and a Chia Pet.

It was an ordinary day and I was flipping through an issue of *Traditional Home* magazine. Then one of those special inserts appeared. It said that if I was interested in receiving information or catalogues about any of the following topics all I had to do was check the boxes, write in an address, and send it off. I began to read the list of subjects which I could request information on: beginning and advanced polka dancing, *The Advocate* (the leading source for lesbian, gay, bi-sexual and straight information), men's swimming fashions, *Karaoke Digest*, women's shoes sizes 11-up, brewing beer in your own bathtub, etc... there was no end to the wealth of knowledge I could get completely FREE. So, I checked all the boxes — including one about using gravity to rid yourself of wrinkles. Now, all I had to do was wait.

It took a couple of weeks. Then the information started to trickle in at my husband's parents' house. I was talking on the phone with my mother-in-law and she said she had gotten a tattoo-start-up kit. Everything you need to know about starting your own tattoo business and getting copyrights for original designs.

"I can't imagine why they sent it to me. I can't even draw a straight line with a ruler," she said. "I only know one person with a tattoo and his motorcycle has teddy bear in the sidecar."

"It's perfect," I said. "You never know when you might have to change professions."

On the next call, my husband's father told me that he was learning welding in his spare time. He'd received some free welding ideas in the mail and was making me a custom set of salt and pepper shakers. Yes, another victory. I had single-handedly expanded Dad's horizons.

Now, there were some rumbles about extra extra-wide women's shoes and bun hugging men's wear over the next few months, but there were rave reviews about *the Chinchilla Source Book*. Because chinchilla's are considered pets, they can be bred in your backyard without raising the hackles of zoning enforcement. A full-length chinchilla coat will have as many as 150 pelts and sells for about $7,000. Mom and Dad were on to something.

They began shopping for chinchillas. Dad was starting to talk about retiring to raise chinchillas. Mom said she had always wanted a chinchilla coat.

They began pricing hutches and food. The start-up chinchilla cost was more than the tattoo one. Then the calls started ... My husband's brother called to say he was concerned about his parents' mental states. "They can't quit their jobs," he said. "The only thing they know about chinchilla farming is what they read on the internet, and Dad still thinks that penny stock he bought in the '70s is going to pay off. Anyway, fur is out. PETA will be wearing down their sidewalk in no time. Mom will be standing at the door in her robe waving off the "20/20" reporter, while Betty White strokes a pet chinchilla on the evening news."

My husband agreed. Chinchilla farming was not for them. When it came time to harvest the animals, Mom and Dad would be like vegetarians on a cattle ranch. We had to stop the chinchilla plans before they began pouring slabs for the cages.

"Why don't you point out to them that the animals have to be sacrificed?" I said.

"Because you know my dad, he thinks he's so macho. That would just make him that much more determined to do it," my husband said, indignantly raising his eyebrows.

"Maybe you and your brother could be conscientious objectors?" I asked.

"And have Dad think we're wimps? No way. We'd never hear the end of it." He was shaking his head now.

"What if you were to suggest that they get allergy tested first? It would just be terrible if they happened to be allergic," I said.

"They're both allergic to dogs but they still have Jake and Taco Bob. I can see that you have no idea how strong-willed my dad can be," my husband said emphatically.

"Why don't you let me see what I can do," I said.

"Aren't you the one who got us into this mess in the first place?"

"Yes, but I've learned my lesson. Let me have a go at it."

"Knock yourself out."

It took a little research, but I finally found a company that trained people on weekends and there was very little initial capital required. "Work with exotic animals. Become an expert, travel, and meet new people," the website said. Mom and Dad love to travel. I contacted the company, told them about Dad, and asked them to send him a brochure.

My husband talked to his dad a week later. "How's the chinchilla farming?" I asked, after he hung up the phone."

"Well, he's found something else that he thinks he could do and still work his day job. It pays a lot better and there's very little start up."

I'd done it. I headed off trouble at the proverbial pass. All it took was a little ingenuity and some research.

"What does your mother think?" I asked, with a satisfied look.

"She thinks snake venom at $2,000 per gram pays much better than chinchillas."

"See, I told you it would work out."

Revenge of the sugar plum fairy

Christmas is always stressful and this year it was no exception. I decked the halls while my son and husband played Halo on the Xbox. My husband said my garlands looked like the letter "U." *Are they not supposed to?*

I attended two Christmas parties and at one of them, my husband issued a last minute invite to two dozen friends and neighbors for the following night.

"I'll need a staging area to serve drinks," he said the next day.

"Here, use this 'bar' on the edge of our kitchen. I've heard it's good for serving things.

And there are these cabinet things above it with glassware," I offered. He was impressed with my ingenuity.

I cajoled my family to attend The Nutcracker. I encouraged the wearing of button-down shirts and shoes that were not flip-flops. I even made my children leave their iPods at home. I watched the delicate, dainty Sugar Plum Fairy with no cellulite dance across the stage. *Oh, I wish I had her thighs and she had my stretch marks.*

I rehearsed for a church play while my husband went to the beach to play with his surfboard. While he was at power yoga in the chair position, I sat hunched over in a chair writing out over a hundred cards. Then I trimmed a thirteen-foot tree as my son updated his Facebook wall with, "Just got a new haircut." Finally, because I was ravenously hungry, I prepared a four-course Christmas dinner for seven. I peeled potatoes while everyone else peeled the plastic off their new gifts. I boiled water for my special deluxe three flavor Jell-O salad, but not until I'd made tea for everyone.

Now, it was the day after the holiday, and I was desperately searching for a missing $300 gift card from, Eric, my only brother. I looked in and around everything in the house. I rummaged under the cushions, in drawers, around the tree, and through the laundry. I discovered dog toys under the sofa, a teeth flosser in the candy dish, and a Chinese fortune cookie in a pot of bamboo, but no plastic gift card.

On Christmas morning, my father-in-law had hurriedly captured all the wrappings and bows — and I suspected a few gifts — and trapped them in garbage bags. So, I finally graduated to the recycling bin. There I found empty wine bottles from the party, the script from the church play, ticket stubs from the ballet, aluminum cans, pie tins, junk mail, newspaper, plastics, and empty Jell-O boxes, but no gift card. The only place I hadn't looked was in the garbage.

Holiday garbage was not an enticing thought. There was the simmered potpourri, the old coffee grounds, and the anatomically correct ham bone — there was nothing appealing about the Ghost of Christmas Past. I put it off for two days — weighing my options. All I had to do was examine the rotting corpse before trash day. Maybe the gift card would show up on its own. Maybe I'd left one rock unturned. Maybe there was a special light that would cause the card to glow when exposed or GPS tracking technology I could access on the internet. Maybe I didn't want to tell my brother I'd lost his Christmas gift. I hated to imagine his response when I asked him to call the store and issue a new card. When we were toddlers, he'd been a biter, I'd learned to give him a wide berth.

I lamented my fate to my family, singing verses of "stale calling curds ... old rubber gloves ... and part-of-a-pear brie." They showed me no sympathy and instead suggested disposable gloves, a flashlight, and theme music. I asked my husband if he had any great ideas. He finally helped me ransack everything in the house that still looked intact. I called my in-laws just to make sure they didn't take it by mistake. I walked the backyard. I emptied my purse. There was no place left to look except in the week of trash that sat lurking, fermenting, molding, and waiting for me to spill its wretched guts. I bowed my head and walked outside toward the den of decay.

Then, a second wish was actually granted. As I was on my knees examining cat litter and egg shells, my husband appeared out of the afternoon sunlight like a gloved superhero and helped me dissect the rest of the decomposing disaster. We opened the nasty, smelly bags and searched. We located banana peels and grapefruit rinds. We reminisced over old tea bags and turkey legs. We found a brand new box of Hello Kitty Band-Aids. We reclassified plastics as recyclable. We talked about episodes of CSI. I mourned the loss of old Christmas bows and broken dishes.

Then we retrieved the last bag in the bottom of the bin. It was a mix of pre-Christmas garbage and "day of" trash. We carefully and dutifully separated each scrap. We were close to the anthropological equivalent of the Jurassic Period when I saw it: the special holiday card my brother had selected just for me—an old guy in Christmas boxers was scratching his rear. I grabbed the card with shaking hands. I held my breath as I opened it. The caption read, "Had to dig deep to get your Christmas gift." *Not as deep as I had to!* And there it was—my gift card. We'd done it.

After twenty years of marriage, my husband and I had found one more thing we were good at. We'd become one. Just like when we first married and then again, when our children were born, we'd had a single purpose. I'd found the one person in the universe who understood me and had a high tolerance for foul odors. It was a cosmic sign. We would be together forever. My life had become as trashy as a soap opera.

Weightloss 101

People are always asking me how I stay in shape. Okay, weight loss is the number one New Year's resolution, right ahead of "stop smoking" and "learn ballroom dancing." According to the Center for Disease Control, 30% of all Americans are overweight and the rest of us are just in denial. But maybe some people just can't imagine their lives without worrying about something. For whatever reason, people have become fixated with the number on the scale. So, after much agonizing, I decided to release my super secret 3-step weight loss technique. Dr. Phil will approve because it has to do with lifestyle changes, but Jenny Craig, eat your heart out, my guaranteed weight loss plan is even successful for those on the Twinkie Diet.

The first and foremost step for any weight loss plan is to set up a healthy environment. This can be the most expensive part of my weight loss secret depending on where you reside. You need to live in at least a two-story residence. This is especially important as you age and find yourself going into a room and forgetting why you went in there. All of the trotting up and down the stairs every time you forget something is worth a loss of at least 10 pounds a year.

The more forgetful you are, the bigger the weight loss. This is a huge boon in middle age. The worse your memory, the more weight you will lose. By the time, dementia has taken its toll and you no longer care how much you weigh, you will have climbed the stairs in your home thousands of times ... You're on your way to the grocery store, and you remember you left your credit card upstairs while you were shopping online — cha-ching, 30 calories burned. You're doing laundry and you remember that the upstairs towels need to be washed — cha-ching, 35 calories. You've carried the downstairs phone upstairs and now its ringing — cha-ching, 30 more calories. You get the picture. You have turned your home into a state-of-the-art gym. Feel free to turn on the television (just like the gym). As you trot around trying to sort out your upstairs-downstairs conundrum, nothing like a little distraction to increase the trips required to complete a simple task. Feel free to turn the TV volume up to blare. Then every time the phone rings, you have to walk into the other room just so you can hear. Cha-ching.

The second requirement also has to do with your environment. You don't have to buy special equipment that will just sit in your bedroom and eventually become a good place to hang laundry. But you will need to buy a standard transmission car and learn how to drive a stick-shift. Even before you implement the shifting, you are making steps toward getting in shape because standard transmissions require a parking brake. Parking brakes require energy. The amount of effort it takes to set a parking brake burns calories. This by itself is exercise.

Of course, now driving requires shifting and shifting burns calories. Shifting requires depressing the clutch with your left leg and wrestling the stick with your right arm. This is far more exercise than you will ever get in your automatic transmission Beemer. It's a little like trying to stuff a cat in a bag. It can be done, but it isn't easy, hence, the remarkable amount of calories burned—more than 55 calories for a simple trip to the store. In stop and go traffic, you might burn up to an extra 75 per hour. If you live someplace that's hilly and has heavy traffic, like San Francisco, you may need to add calories in the form of nutritional supplements to keep up your strength during rush hour.

By the time you have mastered the stick, you are guaranteed to have lost three pounds. And unlike cat-stuffing you have nothing to feel guilty about except when you grind the gears, and your car lets out a huge lurch just to let you know you're an idiot. Within six months your left leg will be worthy of pin-up status. Always position that leg forward when you pose for photos.

The last environmental factor is somewhat more complicated. You will need to adopt a dog, but not just any dog. You will need to adopt a thirsty, indoor dog with a small bladder. Having a dog is crucial to staying in shape. Dogs need to be walked. Chances are your town has a leash law, and you will have to physically take this dog on walks. If you have a yard, even better. Because you will open the door for your pooch, a hundred times a day. Sometimes this will require going down the stairs and dragging open a patio door for a dog who doesn't need to go outside but likes making you come downstairs. Every time you walk to the door to let your urethrallychallenged pooch out, you will burn between 15 to 30 calories depending on the distance. A dog who is fully hydrated will require at least five and up to a hundred door-openings per day. The smaller the bladder, the more calories burned. This technique has also been known to cure sleep disorders. The only time this dog isn't going to need to go outside is when it's asleep. You will learn to relish those few hours when you aren't having to open and close the door for a pet that you adopted from the animal shelter that has to pee every time your soap comes on. You'll now be sleeping like a baby.

If you make these lifestyle changes, I can promise you will begin to see a difference in your metabolism within two weeks. You will start to notice small things, like the huffing and puffing from going up and down the stairs begins to diminish. Your rear-end becomes tight enough to bounce a tennis ball on. One day, you will forget that you hate driving your car and you realize you are making fewer trips to the gas station. Eventually, you stop resenting your dog and take a breath of fresh air every time you open the door.

After the big three changes, you might still want to know what else you can do to burn calories. I hate to mention these next few things because in the wrong hands they are dynamite. Like giving a seagull a sandwich. You must use these techniques with caution.

Are you the "go to person"? This doesn't mean what you think it does? Are you the person who walks to everyone else to carry on a conversation? Does your husband yell at you from his desk or TV and expect you to come running to hear him? Do your children call to you from the kitchen and ask you why the ice-maker isn't working? Do people ask you questions from the bathroom? Being the go-to person burns calories, but it can also have consequences on your sanity. You'll find people trying to carry on conversations from the basement and the yard. Your family will feel free to ask you questions while you are two rooms away carrying in groceries (which also burns calories). Use this technique with caution.

Another way to stay in shape is to park your stick shift automobile across the parking lot and walk. This is also a way to distance yourself from a car you wouldn't otherwise drive.

You'll need extra energy for the additional exercise you will be getting from these last two tips. Caffeine can be your friend if you use caution. Once again, this is a powerful magic. Use it with discretion. And if you overdose on caffeine and start fidgeting, take heart in the knowledge that fidgeting burns calories and fidgetors tend to be thinner.

With a few simple changes, you have re-engineered your health. And who knows, you might eventually sign up your dog up for an obedience class or take up drag racing. You never know where change may lead.

Beep beep

At some point, perhaps in the 80s, it became poor form to yell out the window of your car. "Your mother wears combat boots!" was no longer acceptable traffic etiquette. Maybe because so many mothers actually do wear combat boots — it's lost its punch.

Today, because cars have air conditioning, we use the horn. I don't know exactly what the inventor of the car horn had in mind. Surely, it wasn't safety. Early car horns were known to scare horses and when I was a kid, some people had car horns that played distracting, obnoxious tunes. It wasn't until I moved to a heavily populated area with lots of traffic that I learned about serious beeping.

We all know about the hypnotic spell cast by red lights. We sit there mesmerized, waiting for the light to turn green. We're in a trance. We plan our lives, go over our finances, and inventory the contents of our refrigerators. But not everyone is so easily entranced. I heard about a woman, on her way to a potluck, who made coleslaw at a red light. A friend of mine shaved her legs once. (She said it was an emergency.) Eventually one of these people, whose life is totally squared away, breaks the red-light spell with a short and polite "beep." I don't mind these beeps. They're not angry; they're simply intended to snap us out of our funk and keep traffic flowing at its normal pace.

I have another friend who hates these beeps. She is certain they say, "Wake up and smell the coffee, moron." I, on the other hand, think of them as gentle reminders that we are all human and no one wants to sit through a traffic light for more than one trance. The ones I do resent are the lay-down-on-the-horn honks that say, "I ran out of Prozac a few days ago and I'm on my way to the pharmacy and you're an idiot if you get in my way." Now, while I can appreciate the urgency of the situation, these honks scare the hell out of me. My life flashes before my eyes—especially those ugly scenes when I was trying on swimsuits—and I have no idea what I'm supposed to do. I usually put on the brakes and look around, further frustrating the person behind me whose fondest desire was for me to speed up. It was one of those honks that made me appreciate the importance of sunglasses during traffic altercations.

One day, I was trolling through the parking lot looking for a space when someone in a red Mustang fiercely hit their horn in what was meant to be a—"You stupid idiot, how dare you inconvenience me. Don't you know how to drive?" sort of way. Which prompted me to give them an angry look—one they could not see (or so, I thought) because I was wearing sunglasses. Then I had to drive by them again after they parked because I was still looking for a space. I gave them what my kids call my "stink eye-popping" look—covertly, with sunglasses intact.

I finally parked and was walking into the store when the thirty-something driver of the car who had honked stopped me dead in my tracks. He didn't just walk up to me; he planted himself right in my face.

"What do you think you're doin'?" he spat it out as if I'd just stolen his last French fry. I could feel his hot breath on my cheeks. Now, I was on the defensive. What is it my Karate instructor always says, *"You're in control?"*

"What do you think *you're* doin'?" was the best my creative writer's mind could muster.

"You weren't even watchin' where you were goin'!" he yelled.

I found my 5'7" self looking down at a young, red-faced Don Rickles. He wasn't very tall, a little chubby, no neck and bulged-out, little eyes. An "I'd be angry too if I looked like you," thought ran through my mind, but I dared not say it. After all, plenty of short-necked men were quite successful. Take Dick Chaney for example. Then I noticed that the round-faced little punk had his beige, backward ball cap shoved down pretty far on his head. He looked like one of those pigs-in-a-blanket hors d'oeuvres I make with cocktail sausages around Christmas. His little whiskered mouth area looked like the wrinkly end of the wiener.

"If you hadn't been going so fast, it wouldn't have mattered." Yes, I was clearly going to outthink this guy with my literary prowess.

Honestly, I've never understood the backward ball cap. Backward ball cap guys are always squinting; they remind me of Jackie Chan. Isn't the bill supposed to keep the sun *out* of your eyes? If you have it on backwards, is it to avoid "redneck" sunburns?

This backward-ball-cap-guy was really silly—and inches from my face. I don't know why, but two scenarios flashed through my mind in that instant: I could lean in and lay a big kiss on him to disarm his anger, or I could rip off his cap and throw it as far as possible. I chose the latter and sent his cap flying. As soon as he saw his hat zooming, his little wiener mouth said, "Lady, you're crazy!"

"I'm the crazy one!" I said, strolling into the 99 Cent Store. But the only thoughts in my mind were, "Why do chubby-faced men shave their heads and then put on backward ball caps that make them look even rounder and chubbier?" and "Why didn't he just give me the short beep?"

Galvanized from the parking lot confrontation, I made it my mission to discourage honking. But how? Most people didn't seem conscious of the rudeness of their honking. And how long was I going to be able to thwart honkers who got out of their car and chased me down? My karate lessons would be over soon, and I'd just go back to being a mild-mannered middle-aged woman.

Then it hit me—I remembered the time when an older lady ran a red light right in front of me. It had been one of those trance-like delays, which kept me from a jackrabbit start that prevented a collision. She realized what she had done and actually smiled and waved as she passed by. That's it! I'll smile and wave every time someone honks. What a plan!

From then on, every time someone honked at me, I turned in their direction and smiled my biggest, sincerest grin. If they were behind me, I slowed the shift in my seat a little bit so they had to wait; the longer the honk, the more enthusiastic the wave. It is funny how our facial expression determines our mood. After a particularly heavy traffic session, I came home energized. I'd discovered the cure for road rage. I called it *Honk Therapy*.

I smiled and waved at teenage girls who were texting, I grinned at grumpy contractors on their way to coffee, I even tried my wave/smile combo on a state trooper, who was totally thrown of, and eventually shared a great chicken recipe with me. (The secret is to use a meat injector.) Once when I was walking in a crosswalk and someone honked, I very politely walked up to their car window and asked them if there was an emergency. I even offered to call 911 and pulled out my CPR certification.

I think driver's education should teach beeping etiquette. And traffic schools should definitely have to demonstrate correct beeping. After all, those people are known troublemakers. If it were up to me, I would mandate they all learn about Honk Therapy. It would make the world a better place and my job would be a lot easier.

First car

My daughter had just turned fifteen. She couldn't wait to drive. More importantly, she couldn't wait for us to buy her a Lexus. My husband and I had something much more practical in mind. In fact, we already owned her first car. There was already a 1992 Saturn with 230k miles on the odometer, parked in our driveway right now with her name all over it. (It was written in invisible ink so she could't actually see it.) She assured me that no self-respecting teenager would be caught dead in this car. I assured her, that if she wears her seatbelt and obeys the traffic laws, this should not be a problem.

We are old school. Things like cars and houses should be earned, not manna from heaven. This seemed to fly in face of everything she had seen in high school. We were antiquated, senile and out of touch with reality, she said.

The Saturn was having an intermittent power problem. We had to push-start it every third day. My daughter was embarrassed and humiliated by this process, especially when it happened in the school's parking lot. While we were still in the diagnosis process of finding the electrical glitch. She was in the process of calling Child Protective Services and reporting me for neglect. I couldn't wait until a social worker arrived accusing me of insensitivity to my child's need for speed.

My first car was a 1973 Ford Pinto. It had been involved in an accident and had two dented front fenders and a driver's door that couldn't be opened. I borrowed the $350 for the rolling oven with black interior and no a/c and I was glad to have transportation—any transportation. It was about seven miles to my J-O-B and I had walked on several occasions.

Eventually, I saved up enough money to have the dents repaired and the car repainted. I installed carpet over the factory's vinyl and even had the windows tinted.

Ford recalled the Pinto because it was known to burst into flames after rear end collisions. I never had the recall modification done because I couldn't be without wheels for the two days it would be at the dealership. I continued to drive it. Whenever someone rolled up behind me a little too fast or a little too close, I opened the door—just in case I needed to make a quick getaway away from an exploding gas tank.

It took me to work, to college, to my softball games, to job interviews and more than one bar. Two years later, I sold it for $750. After that, I wore out two Mercedes and put some serious mileage on a Dodge Ram.

The Saturn got about 25 mpg and I didn't have to carry comprehensive or collision insurance on it. One day someone backed into me a knocked quarter size piece of paint off the front end. Their insurance paid me $1300, cha-ching!

I thought the recently painted Saturn was a perfectly respectable car for someone who has never made a single car or insurance payment. I thought it beat walking. I thought cars should be earned and sweated for like homes, facelifts and anything worthwhile. I thought the push start was exercise and parking on a slope was nothing but good planning. My daughter thought I was crazy.

I still have the Saturn. I don't feel guilty about driving it when gas is over five dollars a gallon. But then again, it's no Pinto.